Belief and Misbelief Asymmetry on the Internet

FOCUS SERIES

Series Editor Jean-Charles Pomerol

Belief and Misbelief Asymmetry on the Internet

Gérald Bronner

WILEY

First published in the English language 2016 in Great Britain and the United States by ISTE Ltd and John Wiley & Sons, Inc.
First published in the French language by Presses Universitaires de France, from pages 3–146 and 275–325 (of the French Edition) © *La démocratie des crédules*, Presses Universitaires de France, 2013.

ISTE Ltd
27-37 St George's Road
London SW19 4EU
UK

www.iste.co.uk

John Wiley & Sons, Inc.
111 River Street
Hoboken, NJ 07030
USA

www.wiley.com

Library of Congress Control Number: 2015954428

British Library Cataloguing-in-Publication Data
A CIP record for this book is available from the British Library
ISSN 2051-2481 (Print)
ISSN 2051-249X (Online)
ISBN 978-1-84821-916-8

Contents

Preface

This book will mention the media, beliefs, the news, the Internet, etc. but it should not be seen as yet another critique of the media system, exploring with indignant fascination the idea of a machination against truth set up to serve a society of domination. These kinds of theories, whether they pertain to conspiracy theories or, more subtly, to a self-styled "critical" way of thinking, have always seemed to me the expression of a form of intellectual puerility. This is not to say that attempts at manipulating opinions do not occur, or that our world is free from compromised principles, or indeed corruption; far from it, but none of this is the key issue.

In fact, reality somehow strikes me as even more unsettling than those myths, however sophisticated they might be, which envisage the media system hand-in-hand with industry, science and so forth, all in agreement to lead the "people" away from the truth. This is more unsettling, because the processes that will be described in this book and that allow falsehood and dubiousness to take hold of the public sphere are boosted by the development of IT, the workings of our mind, and the very nature of democracy... It is more unsettling then because we are all responsible for what is going to happen to us.

Introduction: The Empire of Doubt

On December 19th, 2011, I received an email from one of the coordinators of the *Reopen-09/11* website, who claims that the official version of the 9/11 attacks, the one maintaining that those murderous acts were fomented by Al-Qaeda, is questionable. If he wrote to me, it is due to the fact that, on several occasions, I have had the opportunity to show in newspapers, on the radio and even on television, how the mechanisms of belief we call conspiracy theories were at work. As it happens, I have sometimes taken as an example those individuals believing that these attacks have been organized by the CIA. There would be many things to say about that very polite email, if only about this apparently innocent and very sensible question he asked me: "Don't you think that an independent investigation would once and for all allow those who believe the accredited version and those who are in doubt to come to an agreement?" This question suggested that the official report [NAT 04] had been written by dubious experts and it gave the impression, as often happens when an "independent" assessment is required, that my interlocutor wouldn't be satisfied unless that assessment eventually yielded a report that would substantiate his theories. It so happened that what mostly drew my attention was the heading of his email: "right to doubt", which indicated that its sender felt one of his basic rights had been scoffed at.

It may be surprising that this gentleman claims a right that, ostensibly, he already fully exerts. Did anyone prevent him from coordinating that website, posting videos on the Internet, publishing books, writing articles, handing out pamphlets in the street, organizing public demonstrations and generally making his voice heard? Once this question has been asked, it is possible to admit to him that in fact the right to doubt is fundamental if only because, without this right, human knowledge could not rectify itself. If the scientific world were deprived of this right, for example, it would be impossible to envisage any advances in knowledge: the leading scientific theories would be deemed immutable and human progress would come to a halt, not to mention, naturally, the consequences the lack of this right has in the political field. But what this gentleman does not seem to realize when claiming this "right to doubt" is that, as is often the case with rights, it implies some duties.

Why duties? Because a doubt which intends to exist for its own sake and completely unrestrainedly can easily become a sort of mental nihilism, a negation of any discourse. It is possible to show that something exists, but it is impossible to show definitively that something does not exist. Now, this is precisely what the over-suspicious demands from any official utterance: show me that there is no conspiracy, show me that this product does not pose any danger... I can prove that horses exist, but I cannot prove that unicorns do not exist. If I claim that no one has ever seen them and that the existence of such a creature would be contrary to zoological knowledge, someone who mistrusts the official truth will easily be able to object, stating that science has often been mistaken in its history and that perhaps unicorns exist in unchartered territories, deep in thick forests, on other planets, etc. He will even be able to provide first-hand accounts of people claiming to have seen some, to produce some marks one of them might have left...

This is an example of that sort of sophism called *argumentum ad ignorantiam*, the appeal to ignorance.

As we will see, the conditions themselves of our contemporary democracy favor, on the one hand, the propagation of this *argumentum ad ignorantiam* through the public sphere and, on the other hand, the possibility for the person claiming the right to doubt to bury any rival discourse under a plethora of arguments. To return to the 9/11 example, let us remember that the conspiracy myth is supported by nearly a hundred different arguments, some having to do with material physics, some others with seismology or with stock market analysis [ANF 10]!

This situation will engender a mental maze with no easy way out for those who have no specific opinion on a given subject and, whether they subscribe to this obsessive distrust or not, they will be left with a sense of discomfort.

Generally speaking, when it comes to a number of questions, such as those concerning public health, environmental issues, economic topics, the exercise of political power, the spreading of information in conventional media, etc., a doubt seems to gnaw at our contemporaries.

This right to doubt seems to have become so invasive that those who lay claim to it as a kind of moral intimidation seem to forget about the existence of the abuse of rights. We will remind those people who may find this observation repressive that, on the one hand, nothing is more restrictive than freedom exerted unrestrainedly, and that on the other hand, the possible impact of this metastatic doubt goes way beyond the irritation it provokes in a sensible mind. Actually, if we think about it for a moment, the essence of any social life is confidence.

If we can live with one another, it is because we have the impression that a certain predictability characterizes communal living. Thus, when Mr A goes out to work, he hopes he will not be a robber or an assassin's victim; when he buys his cinema ticket, he expects the operators to project the programmed movie; during green time at the traffic lights, when he drives on confidently, he assumes that the drivers on the road perpendicular to him will respect the traffic rules; and he hopes, with good reason, that his letter, once mailed, will find its recipient due to a chain of actions carried out by workers he knows pretty much nothing about.

Many of these predictions are implicit (if it were otherwise, our mind would be overwhelmed by the mass of information it would need to process), because they are based on the experience of individuals who can, on average, rely on this predictability of social order: they are confident. This confidence is a very strong conviction, since it is based on an important aggregate of experiences, but it is also precarious, being only a belief. In order to exist, every social order needs this confidence to be shared extensively. It only takes several people to start doubting whether the others will stop at the red light for everyone to slow down at every junction and create traffic jams in cities. In general, it seems that the level of distrust toward political power is related to the mistrust of others which characterizes a population, as is shown by the large international survey by Ingelhart and his colleagues [ING 03]. Just to take one example, Brazil, one of those countries where mistrust of politics is strongest, is also the motherland of person-to-person distrust, since only 2.8% of Brazilians declare that they generally trust others. The consequences that the alteration of this belief brings about may be more dire. So, if in a highly tense political climate, it is rumored that some gunshots have been fired in town, a certain number of people may decide to stay indoors in order not to risk being exposed to the acts of violence of a sudden civil war. By doing this, they will help substantiate the idea that grave events are brewing, and will enter a cumulative vicious circle.

This is what might have happened in India on the November 20th, 1984 when in New Delhi rumors that President Zail Singh had been killed began circulating. Throughout the eight hours before the evening news, the city lived in a state of fear that the false piece of information could not have failed arousing. Traumatized as it was by the recent murder (October 31st 1984) of Indira Gandhi, public opinion was that Indian society was fragile and highly unstable. In these circumstances, a new political assassination might have had tragic social effects. Government workers, bank employees and some school professors left their workplace earlier than they were supposed to, whereas storekeepers pulled down their metal shutters and the switchboards of press agencies were deluged. Social order was threatened since everyone, ignoring what others were going to do, could see the mechanism of his or her daily predictions stop working. This rumor was dispelled once the evening news showed images of the President safe and sound, receiving visitors, and attending to his affairs. The anchor, who was aware of the rumor, underscored in his commentary that the President was perfectly fine.

What happened exactly? There had actually been a murder at the presidential palace, but it was that of a gardener. In the sociopolitical context of India, the natural interpretation was that, had an assassination taken place at the palace, it certainly had to be the President's. The city got off lightly that day, but no flight of fancy is needed to imagine how the situation might have ended differently. Confidence is thus necessary to any social life but it is also essential for this other reason, which specifically concerns democratic societies, pivoted around the progress of knowledge and the division of intellectual work which is its direct consequence. Actually, the extent to which each can hope to master this shared competence diminishes in rapport with the production of this knowledge. In other terms, the more someone knows, the less important *my* share of knowledge proportionally becomes. No one denies the fact that although a few centuries ago someone could master all of sciences, this could not be possible today. This means that a kind of society based on the progress of knowledge becomes, quite paradoxically, a society of *delegated belief*, hence of confidence, which is what Tocqueville had written in his time: "There is no such great philosopher in this world that he does not believe a million things about the faith of others, and who does not assume many more truths than he establishes. This is not only necessary, but desirable" [TOC 92]. Indeed desirable because we cannot envisage a world that could survive for long, had everyone to verify frenetically every bit of information. There are however certain social conditions where this process of *confidence* is altered.

Western democracies are not, of course, in the same circumstances of political tension India was at the beginning of the 80s. We do not seem to be on the verge of a civil war, but in every sphere, the questioning of authority and the official word, and mistrust of the experts' findings are tangible. For example, the results of the different polls about distrust are at the best of times ambiguous, and in the worst case frankly worrying. For example, a survey[1] on the feelings of the French about science, carried out in 2011, yielded contrasting results, some of which however betrayed that doubt about major issues gnawing at people. So, when replying to the question: "Do science and technology cause more harm than good?", 43% answered "yes". We may rejoice that 56% still reply "no" (and 1% "are undecided"), and that we find again the same percentages for the question: "Are future generations going to live better than present-day ones due to science and technology?". However, we can also come to understand that that question is the expression of incredible ingratitude. Do those who have replied to those questions fully realize that life expectancy at birth was barely 30 years old in 1800 and that it was timidly reaching 60 at the beginning of 1960s, whereas it nowadays exceeds 80?[2] Do they know that the average temperature inside a London apartment in the 19th Century was 12°C? Have they forgotten about the plague epidemics or outbreaks of cholera or typhus which have killed millions of people? Do they not appreciate on a day-to-day basis the benefits of electricity, electronics or informatics?

This mistrust of science, which has been growing for around 30 years[3], becomes even more evident when certain subjects, which have received a lot

---

1 A survey by Ipsos – Logica Business Consulting – *La Recherce* and *Le Monde* can be found at: http://www.larecherche.fr/content/system/media/Rapport.pdf.
2 http://www.ined.fr/fr/tout_savoir_population/graphiques_mois/esperance_vie_france.
3 http://www2.cnrs.fr/presse/journal/1715.htm.

of media attention and thus seem well-known to people, are tackled: for example, 58% affirm that they do not consider scientists to be truthful when it comes to genetically-modified organisms (GMOs) or nuclear energy (only 33 and 35%, respectively, have trust in them). Furthermore, 72% believe that the assessment of the safety of nuclear plants cannot be reliable. I know at this stage of their reading, many of those who are running their eyes over these lines will find these positions to be sensible and will not realize how doubt, expressed as such, can be excessive. If this were not the case, this book would be purposeless. As I will also say later, genetically-modified organisms(GMOs) appropriately exemplify the way falsehood has taken hold of public opinion. The perception of biotechnologie has changed throughout Europe since the beginning of 1990s [BOY 03].

This suspicion is not limited to science. Journalists, who are supposed to keep citizens informed, do not get a better deal[4]. Respondents actually think that journalists are not immune to pressure exerted by political parties or power 63% of the time and from buy-offs in 58% of circumstances. Television, which still remains the main source of information in Western countries[5], has lost nearly 20 points in confidenced since 1989: for example, nowadays, in France, 54% of people think that reality does not correspond (either exactly or approximately) to what is presented on television. Similarly, in the United States, 60% of Americans distrust the media[6].

As for politicians[7], respondents affirm that they only have confidence in 42% of cases and, if mayors get a slightly better deal than others with 54%, deputies only receive 30%. Besides, more than one person out of two does not trust politicians whatsoever, whether they are right- or left-wing, to govern the country and only 30% deem politicians to be generally quite honest. It is scarcely any better in the United States where 74% of Americans have no faith in government actions in general[8].

While this survey attempts to grasp the state of mind of citizens, the results are not any more encouraging: weariness, gloominess and fear are

4 A TNS-Sofres survey carried out by *La Croix*, available at: http://tns-sofres. com/_assets/files/2011.02.08-baro-media-pdf.
5 As much in Europe as in the USA: http://www.gallup.com/poll/163412/americans-main-source-news.apx.
6 http://www.politico.com/news/stories/0912/81504.html.
7 Cevipof 2011 survey: http://www.cevipof.com/fr/le-barometre-de-la-confiance-politique-du-cevipof/resultats3/.
8 http://www.people-press.org/2014/11/13/public-trust-in-government/.

growing whereas serenity, enthusiasm and wellbeing are dropping (in relation to the previous poll carried out in 2010). However, the term that has most noticeably increased is *distrust*: +6%, encompassing 34% of respondents. More generally, 70% think we are never too cautious when dealing with others and 38% that most people try to take advantage of others.

In general, individuals' trust in their political institutions has weakened a little everywhere [DON 05]. These kinds of results may be obtained in a number of Western countries, where unease is often a source of national distress. The last study by the Gallup International association, carried out in 2012 in 51 countries to measure the "morale" of different peoples, shows that somewhat paradoxically these ills do not spare the richest countries. We may well say that money does not make us happy but let us admit that it is nonetheless perplexing to realize this poll shows that French people, for example, affirm they are less optimistic than Nigerians or Iraqis, whose countries are threatened by famine and civil war. Besides the explanations that clarify these surprising results, it is rather shameful to see the predominant expression of a point of view which resembles that of a spoiled brat.

Those living in stable democracies, and whose freedom and safety are guaranteed, do not feel satisfied and appear to be looking for a way to be the *victim* of something. The victim status, as Erner has shown [ERN 06], has paradoxically become enviable in the democratic sphere. That doubt gnawing at us is able to offer everyone victim status: most often a victim of the powerful, who plot a machination against truth. For if this mistrust may be merely a widespread feeling, it may also structure itself into a condemning discourse. This is exactly what happens with the different conspiracy theories that seem to be making big comeback in the public sphere these last few years[9]. What do they consist of? A paranoid universe which can be defined by such expressions as: "everything is linked", "nothing happens by accident", or again "things are not what they seem." The DSK case, Illuminati, the attacks of 9/11, the earthquake in Haiti, our rulers replaced by lizard men, floods, etc. From the most bizarre topics to the most troublesome, the conspiratorial imagination presents the idea that some forces prevent us from knowing the world as it is, that some things are hidden from us. Considered as such, it is another expression of that mistrust which is spreading everywhere.

---

9 [CAM 05] [TAG 05] or [CHA 05]: the fact that these three books were published in the same year is a mark of the resurfacing of these themes.

Conspiracy myths are ever-recurring phenomena for the human imagination. First of all, because they conspicuously help our thirst for knowledge. These myths are based on a *revelatory effect* which really satisfies our mind, a sentiment resembling what we feel when we find out the answer to a riddle: it is a matter of giving coherence to facts which were up to then disjointed, of finding a link between apparently independent events by showing that they are tied together, behind the scenes, by a group or an individual's will. These myths are often speculative and thus easily stay in our minds. Subsequently they are easily memorized, which constitutes a major advantage for their propagation through the cognitive market. What is more, the endorser of a conspiracy theory feels that his knowledge is somewhat superior to his fellow's and that he is consequently less naive. Hence the fact that it is not always easy to convince him about the futility of his arguments, since he sees his interlocutor as the mediator of an official doctrine that needs fighting. If we add to this that conspiracy myths often flatter stereotypes or every form of subculture, it is easy to understand that we need not be irrational in order to find them appealing.

Examples of conspiracy myths are present throughout history: the Protocols of the Elders of Zion, the notion that the French Revolution was fomented by Freemasons... The regulations of the Templars' trial itself could be seen as the set of laws of a conspiracy theory. Many events, be they fictitious or real, which cannot be explained intuitively, are liable to generate a conspiracy myth. The 20th Century has not been spared by this: Jews, Freemasons, gypsies, etc. have been, one by one or together, part of stigmatised groups, judged responsible for every kind of calamity: unemployment, cholera, inflation, political scheming, manipulation of opinions, etc. Therefore conspiracy theories were not born in the 21st Century, but nowadays seem to win over an unprecedented audience. Just to take one example, is it not bewildering, poll after poll, to observe the success of the 9/11 conspiracy theories? It may not be surprising[10] to see that it is in Arab countries where this myth finds more resonance insomuch as it is generally not Americanophilia or Israelophilia which characterise them (thus 55% of Egyptians and nearly one Jordanian out of two think these attacks were instigated by the United States or Israel), but it is astounding to realize that this belief is quite popular in several Western countries such as Germany, where the rate of those in favor of conspiracy still reaches 26%. The most worrying results are undoubtedly those obtained in the United

---

10 The results presented here come from a survey carried out in 2008 in 17 countries by WorldPublicOpinion.org.

States themselves, since a survey shows that 36% of Americans affirm they deem it possible or even very likely that federal officials have been involved in the attacks[11].

As observed by Campion-Vincent [CAM 05], while we thought the conspiratorial imagination to be confined to the reactionary way of thinking, it now seeps down through every layer of the populace, way beyond merely political themes. The second aspect of our contemporary conspiratorial way of thinking, she explains, consists of imagining the existence of "megaplots", i.e. machinations with planetary ambitions. Everything happens as if imaginary themes, like pretty much everything else, became globalized. Some of these myths easily provoke mockery, as when David Icke, obsessed with lizards, envisages our great politicians as "were-reptiles" who descend from an ancient Sumerian-extraterrestrial race, or again when some defend the myth of the "chemtrails", affirming that the wakes left by planes in the sky are chemicals designed by governments to manipulate the weather or minds. Some other times, they lead events to their bloody outcomes like in the Waco tragedy or in the murderous attack of Oklahoma City.

It is another reason to find their recent success disturbing.

Contemporary conspiracy theories, however different they may look, seem to converge toward a joint denunciation: the categories of collective anxiety have changed over recent decades. The example of John Fitzgerald Kennedy's assassination emerges emblematically from this panorama (75% of Americans nowadays affirm that they side with conspiracy theories in this matter). Who is responsible for this murder? Answers differ: the KKK, aliens, the mafia, etc. but the culprit which hauntingly recurs over and over again is the CIA. The implication of the American governmental agency is not actually insignificant, since now it is seen as the ideal offender for any kind of plot, representing as it does the poisonous side of American power. Two malevolent and scheming entities emerge from the contemporary imagination when it comes to conspiracy: science and, more generally, Western governments and their secret services, often hand-in-hand with the media as an accomplice. Previously the ideal culprits were mostly outsiders or minorities, i.e. *the others*, which might have led to terrible consequences as history has shown, but imaginary fears offer new actors for the theatre of hatred and these actors may well be another version of *ourselves*, as the expression of a form of self-hatred, since science, as well as our rulers and the media, are emblems of Western contemporariness.

---

11 http://www.scrippsnews.com/911poll.

The West, willing to bend nature and other peoples to its illogical and immoral desires, becomes the ideal culprit. For these conspiracy theories chance is an unwelcome guest, since they claim to expose the coherence of disparate elements of human history while denouncing those responsible for the misfortunes of the world. In this sense, the complexity of reality is always rejected in favor of the search for the single cause and we may as well worry about how the contemporary way of thinking sees in doubt and generalized suspicion a sign of intelligence rather than a weakness in discernment.

Once again, when it comes to knowing whether or not Barack Obama was teleported to Mars when he was 19 years old by an American secret agency which wanted to colonize the red planet, as affirmed by Andrew D. Basiago and William Stillings, two self-styled "chrononauts", we cannot help being amused. Although we may ask whether it was necessary to provide a refutation, if ironical, to this hypothesis, as the White House did in January 2012. It is undoubtedly more disquieting when this suspicion focuses on medical competence and, for example, leads vaccination coverage for such diseases as hepatitis B or measles to fall, thus resulting in deaths whose victims will ignore being casualties of this generalized suspicion. The case of the MMR (measles, mumps and rubella) vaccine is exemplary and appalling.

At the end of the 90s, *The Lancet*, an English medical journal, was as thoughtless as to publish a study claiming to show links between this vaccine and the occurrence of certain pathologies, especially autism [KRI 10]. Later developments showed how this article, based on only 12 cases, was untrustworthy, and its conclusions were contradicted several times by expansive studies that attempted in vain to replicate the results that had been presented. *The Lancet* and several authors of that article recanted, the editor-in-chief of the medical journal even declared to *The Guardian*: "It is perfectly clear and unmistakable that the declarations made in this study are completely false. I feel deceived".

The whole incident led to a condemnation of the British Medical Council, but it would be a mere anecdotal episode at most, were it not that it engendered a significant drop in vaccine coverage and a resurgence in cases of measles in several countries. Nowadays, years after that incident, rumors are still being circulated and parents are reluctant to expose their children to what they consider "a vaccine-related risk". We could say the same about the vaccine for hepatitis B, which still carries with it the rumor that it may favour the development of multiple sclerosis, and stirs up a certain reluctance in people which is not endorsed by the medical community. This is another case where we can expect, in future generations, numerous patients to consider themselves destined to be victims, unaware they were instead victims of their parents' thoughtless suspicion.

This suspiciousness, whether explicit or implicit, has always existed – it is the prerogative of power, be it economic, political, or symbolic to provoke these kinds of feelings – and has gone hand-in-hand with democracy from its origins and throughout its history [ROS 06].

However, as we have seen, this doubtfulness has reinvented itself as for its themes and the objects it projects itself onto, and above all it has propagated well beyond the lands of radicalism which, until recently, were the only significant spaces where it could find fertile ground.

It is difficult to come to grips with a phenomenon as substantial as that by citing people's stupidity or their dishonesty, as often happens when one is faced with beliefs he or she finds disconcerting. What then? I will take the opposite direction and I will start from the hypothesis that the situation is quite the reverse, since people have *reasons* to believe what they believe[12] and it is thanks to arguments particularly sound at first sight that this current doubt is gaining ground. To have *reasons* to believe does not mean that someone is *right* to believe, but that what leads us to agree, in addition to our desires and emotions, is coherence, argumentative power, and the coincidental fact that people want us to consider misleading propositions, claiming to shed light on the world, as facts. What is revealed by these propositions is the *dark side of our rationality.*

In this book, we will see that it is the new conditions of the information market and the incursion of doubt and falsehood into our public space which favor the expression of this dark side of our rationality. No one is especially responsible for this situation, not journalists, not scientists, not politicians, not Internet users, not even the conspiracy theorists themselves! It is a matter of shared responsibilities. To shed light on the situation we find ourselves in, I will show that it derives from a double process of "deregulation": the

---

12 I draw inspiration from Raymond Boudon's position about this point [BOU 95] and more recently (2012), who herself draws from German sociologist Max Weber.

liberalization of the information market (the media, whatever their relationships, can start competing) and the offer revolution on this same market (anyone can propose a "product" on the information market). This twofold process reflects the two main values of our societies: freedom and equality, and it is thus awkward for me, being a democrat, to conceive it as inherently bad. On the other hand, everyone is allowed to show that it produces certain perverse effects so formidable that I am not afraid to write that it is defining the outline of a historic, if deeply unsettling, moment for our democracies. It is throwing a spanner in the redoubtable works that lead certain inaccurate ways of thinking to be made public, whereas they formerly remained private. This dark side of rationality is going to take hold of the democratic mind. Maybe it is not too late. It is as a lover of democracy that I have written this book, thus it really mattered to me, after a possibly frightening diagnosis, to take action and offer some solutions, not exclusively radical, to the problem.

1

More is Less: Mental Avarice and Mass Information

1.1. The revolution of the cognitive market

The cognitive market is a metaphor that allows us to envisage the fictitious space through which cognitive products, such as hypotheses, beliefs, knowledge, etc., spread. It will be preferred to the *information market* metaphor, since a piece of information may as well be the address of a restaurant or someone's phone number, whereas the notion of cognitive product will imply, in the sense I will attribute to it here, the organizing of information into a discourse, whether explicit or implicit, on truth and/or on what is good. These cognitive products can be in competition with one another as are, for example, the literal description given by the Bible about the first appearance of man and animals on the Earth and their oldness, *with* the rival interpretation advanced by the theory of evolution. According to the biblical text, and specifically Genesis (1: 20-30 and 2: 7), animals and man were created by God, each species was created separately, the Earth was made in 6 days (Genesis 1: 1-31) and it should be 6,000 years old. Fossil finds, their dating, the interpretation that puts forward the theory of evolution and, generally, the progress of knowledge over the last two centuries have made the biblical vision of the world, predominant for hundreds of years, very impractical. It is possible to say that these two cognitive products are still in *competition* (especially in the United States).

The cognitive market may be very competitive but, on the contrary, it may also be oligopolistic, not to say monopolistic. The market liberalization depends on several criteria, the political one being the most evident. Totalitarian regimes always entail the supervision of the cognitive market, or at least of some of its themes. Thus, it will be difficult to express Christian beliefs if the Talibans are in power. However, cognitive oligopolies may also exist within democracies, this time not because of political constraints, but because truth seems so evident that competing products are completely unsuccessful. So, the notion that the Earth is flat is not a very engaging product in contemporary society[1].

The Internet – I will often bring this up – is the appropriate tool for a deregulation of the cognitive market. Thus, the cognitive market belongs to a family of social phenomena (which also includes the economic market), where individual interactions converge, more or less unquestionably, toward relatively steady forms of social life. The word *market* is not, it goes without saying, neutral. It has a long history that a few trace back to Aristotle [DEF 95], whereas many associate its origins with Smith or Turgot. My aim is not to apply this term to the universe of human cognition by seeking "word-for-word" applications for those realities that are common on the economic market. On the contrary, I had the opportunity to show some of the limits of this metaphor [BRO 03], but the fact remains that its descriptive qualities are very helpful for defining the phenomena at stake here.

We can say that the first appearance of language in human history is the *sine qua non* of the subsistence of a cognitive market. As for writing, since it hinders the semantic volatility of every conversation, it has been a fundamental stage in preparation for this revolution of cognitive supply, which characterizes 21st Century democracies. However, the beginning of a kind of cognitive supply intended for a gradually increasing public can be traced back[2] to the 15th Century, when typography and printing became operational, and to the 17th Century, when the first important periodicals appeared. On this account, Luther's will to translate the New Testament into a vernacular language (and not into Latin) in 1524 favors the access for most people to a source of information deemed fundamental at the time. If such bibles existed before, they were manuscripts and consequently unaffordable, besides being condemned by the Vatican.

---

1 But, it is nonetheless "put forward" since the members of the Flat Earth Society claim that our planet is disk-shaped, with the North Pole as its center and Antarctica as its circumference. And since no one would ever cross Antarctica, no one would ever fall off the disk. See http://www.lepcf.org/wiki.
2 All of what follows draws from [ALB 03, CAR 10, FLI 10] and [POU 11].

Nonetheless, the development of printing in the 17th and 18th Centuries occured under the yoke of censorship, which provoked people's mistrust and perpetuated the appeal of the manuscripts circulating from town to town and that of precious books, less liable to be controlled by political and religious powers. The following centuries were marked by the progressive liberalization of supply, first in England and then in France at the time of the Declaration of the Rights of Man in 1789, which proclaims that "the free communication of thoughts and opinions is one of the most precious rights Man has; every citizen can talk, write, and print freely". Censorship is an ever-recurring phenomenon in the history of the diffusion of information and ideas, but it will soon be outflanked by technical innovations (cylindrical press, rotary printing press, linotype, etc.) which will bring down the price. It will also shrink down due to the democratic injunctions that pepper the 20th Century.

The 19th Century is marked by the first sharp increase in the circulation of information, supported by a now overabundant supply of periodicals. Simultaneously, people's growing literacy ensured favorable conditions for the appearance of a demand that grow global and automatically boosted the strength of supply.

The 20th Century was evidently a turning point in the history of this revolution of supply. From this point of view, 1898 is a significant date since it is when, for the first time, a piece of information was transmitted independently from corded technology. On November 5 of that year, Eugène Ducretet transmitted a message in Morse code from the Eiffel Tower to the Pantheon. Cognitive supply took a crucial step: it cut loose from the spatial and temporal constraints that burdened it. It was from the Eiffel Tower itself that the first program was broadcast in France. We had to wait until 1921, but this message, rather than being transmitted in Morse code, was broadcast in a language everyone could hear, which lasted half an hour and included a press review, a weather report and a piece of music. At this moment in time, demand was technically limited insofar as few people owned radio sets, but soon a number of households were equipped and this demand increased massively, whereas the supply remained feeble (in England, for example, the BBC was in a position of monopoly until 1955). 1926 saw the first appearance of the technology that would radically change over the course of the 20th Century the history of cognitive supply: the television. However, we had to wait until 1930 for the marketing of the first popular television set (the first regular TV program was offered from 1935 onward) and many more years before every household had one.

In France, despite the 1923 bill (which forced those who owned radio sets to declare it officially), the existence of private radio was tolerated, but World War II ended this liberal approach and re-established, from 1945, a strict State monopoly of French radio broadcasting and, naturally, television. The first use of FM broadcasting, which allowed us to technically augment supply, in 1954 would later occasion a shift in policy of the State monopoly.

In the meantime, in 1961, MIT student Leonard Kleinrock, with Joseph Licklider's contribution, laid the theoretical foundations of what would later become the Internet. This was the epilogue of the Arpanet project, conceived in 1968, that advanced a system of networked dissemination of information that could get round the damage provoked by a nuclear attack. Soon afterward, this network started developing more in US West Coast universities than in military bases, especially over the following year, linking Columbia, Stanford, the University of Utah and the University of California to a network allowing a data sharing speed of up to 50 kbits/s.

Simultaneously, and progressively, cognitive supply developed, and, in France for example, in 1972 the third television channel was created. It is true that only a quarter of French people could receive it, but this represented another step toward the introduction of supply competition. We still had an illiberal system of State monopoly but the dismantling of the *office de radiodiffusion-télévision française* (ORTF) in 1975 announced the end of this era. In this audiovisual panorama, the creation of CNN, the first television channel without interruption, by Ted Turner, was a significant step. A year later, France took a crucial step toward the deregulation of the cognitive market by authorizing public radio. Supply became cacophonic, but Darwinian selection shows year after year the nature of the demand that defines the radio landscape as we know it today. This point is important since the audience of the time, which regulated demand, was confronted with a really wide range of offers and the aggregation of this supply has shaped the nature of the radio market. No one who experienced this age could say that the audience was conditioned to ask for mediocrity rather than for challenging products. The evolution itself of these radio stations, such as NRJ and Fun Radio, says a great deal about the kinds of adjustments made by the supply to meet the demand.

In 1986, the French television market opened to private supply with Silvio Berlusconi's *La 5*. Soon, it became really competitive with the privatization of *TF1* in 1987 and the appearance of M6. The former became the first French general-interest channel, whereas the latter, on some evenings, objected to its title. In the meantime, in the United States, *the Well*

(Whole Earth 'Lectronic Link), which represents the prototype of all those forums of virtual discussion we are so familiar with nowadays, was founded in 1985. Some years later, in 1989, Tim Berners-Lee's work started outlining the "Web", as it became known. In the United States, the Internet enterprise started taking the shape of something with the potential to affect the general public in the 1990s, with the appearance of the first browsers and search engines. Netscape, for example, first got listed on the stock market in 1995. We know what happened afterward, in 1995 there were 23,500 Websites, more than 205 million were listed in 2010. Like radio or television, the Internet quickly conquered households all over the world in developed or emerging countries, creating demand in the same way literacy had formerly been an important condition for the development of the cognitive market. The Internet represents a double revolution, as Cardon writes [CAR 10, p.11]: "On the one hand, the right to speak publicly is extended to the whole of society; on the other, a part of private conversation is incorporated into public space".

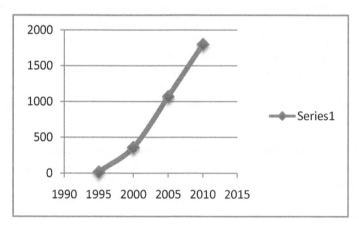

Figure 1.1. *Number of Internet users (in millions) across the globe*

What makes the Internet possible is thus a revolution of cognitive supply. In France, the July 29th, 1881 bill on freedom of the press allowed professionals to have a monopoly of the diffusion of public information. They operated a selection between the flux of information that could be diffused and the one that had to, according to depreciation standards everyone could understand. This filter no longer exists and the opportunity to provide supply on the cognitive market has been radically democratized. Millions of people manage a blog and more than 2 billion of them are on social networks. For example, Indymedia, proposing a summary of this Web potential, has adopted the slogan: "Do not hate the media, become the media!" This Website is in fact pivoted around the principle of "open publishing". Gradually, on the Internet, the idea of an *a posteriori* form of editorial control has established itself, as can be found on Wikipedia, OhmyNews or Agoravox, contrary to the standard *a priori* control that had up to then prevailed in the traditional media. Before this supply revolution, which concretized the Internet, access to the public space was very strict and socially discriminating but, as we will see, the door has opened so wide that the usual rules of sensible debate are sometimes carried away with the stream. Simultaneously, as stated by Poulet [POU 11, p. 23, p. 50], this supply revolution goes hand-in-hand with a decline in the number of traditional formats for the dissemination of information: in the United States, we find, in 2008, no more than 53 million newspaper buyers, whereas there were 62 million in 1970 and, he explains, "if we take into account the population increase, that represents a 74% drop". The situation is identical in France – and a bit everywhere – and for that matter big general-interest radio stations and even the main TV channels see tens of thousands of viewers walking away from their screen every year. We may argue that this change in the format of dissemination and reception of information is not really important, were it not that this transformation also affects the nature of distributed information. Poulet sensibly shows that this global movement is automatically accompanied by the impoverishment of the quality of information.

It is then the simultaneity of political and technical conditions that has made this revolution of the cognitive marked possible. Its many consequences only started being gauged recently: price drop in information distribution and acquisition, mass supply, increase in competition between distributors of information, etc.

1.2. Amplification of the confirmation bias

The cognitive market of contemporary Western societies is globally liberal to the extent that, with few exceptions (for example, the interdiction of Holocaust denial), products are not subjected to state tax or prohibition. This cognitive liberalism is an integral part of the constitution of democracies itself, and we saw that in 1789 it had been regarded as a fundamental Human right. This cognitive liberalism is authorized by political decisions and made possible by technological advances. From this point of view, the Internet is its emblematic manifestation. This political and technological liberalization of the cognitive market inevitably leads to mass-distributed information. Thus, some research [AUT 02] has claimed that the amount of worldwide information produced *over 5 years* at the end of the 20th and at the beginning of the 21st Century was quantitatively superior to *the entirety of the information printed since Gutenberg*. Let us remember that in 2005, humankind produced 150 exabits of data, a number that goes up to 1,200 in 2010. In brief, a large amount of information is disseminated and in such proportions that it is already a major turning point in human history. But basically, what difference does all of that make? There is more and more information available. All the better for democracy and all the better for knowledge, which will of course end up forcing itself on everybody's mind.

This perspective seems too optimistic to me. It presupposes that, in this open competition between beliefs and systematic knowledge, the latter will necessarily gain the upper hand. Now, faced with this overabundant market supply, a person may easily be tempted to form an opinion of the world that tends to be more mentally handy than truthful. In other words, the plurality of offers available to this person will allow him or her to easily avoid the mental discomfort often generated by the products of knowledge. This discomfort may be the consequence of many things.

On the one hand, these products are often more complex than their competitors and, in order to be completely and properly understood, they need technical and theoretical competences that are often beyond the scope of common sense, even in their popularized forms. Many get discouraged in advance when faced with a scientific utterance and eventually only agree to listen to its conclusions to better and more rapidly forget about them and to accept more accessible interpretations of these phenomena. Consequently, certain unscientific or pseudoscientific explanations seem more convincing since, besides being themselves well argued, they are inspired by a kind of logic that can be grasped at once by the interlocutor.

On the other hand, the products of knowledge may easily arouse a form of disenchantment since the models they offer for understanding the world are based on mechanisms rather than magic tricks or transcendental wills whose existence could assure us that the universe makes sense.

Simultaneously, the products of belief pander to the natural inclinations of our mind. The revolution of the cognitive market therefore organizes a wildly competitive space. This competition, besides being ruthless, is quite unfair.

I have just mentioned such terms as "mental easiness", mind inclinations... how are we supposed to interpret them? The explosion of supply facilitates the *pluralist* presence of cognitive offers on the market and their greater *accessibility*. Nowadays, everyone can easily subscribe to a representation of the world drawing some of its elements from Christianity, some others from Buddhism and some others again from conspiracy theories, all the while believing that our health is governed by waves and claiming, however, to somehow be a rational being. The least noticeable consequence, and yet the more determining for this state of affairs, is that all these conditions are gathered together allowing the *confirmation bias* to show its potential to lead us away from the truth. Out of all the inferential temptations that trouble ordinary logic, the confirmation bias is undoubtedly the most influential for the perpetuation of beliefs. It is described as early as aphorism 46 of Bacon's *Novum Organum*:

> "The human understanding when it has once adopted an opinion (either as being the received opinion or as being agreeable to itself) draws all things else to support and agree with it. And though there be a greater number and weight of instances to be found on the other side, yet these it either neglects and despises, or else by some distinction sets aside and rejects; in order that by this great and pernicious predetermination the authority of its former conclusions may remain inviolate. And therefore it was a good answer that was made by one who when they showed him hanging in a temple a picture of those who had paid their vows as having escaped shipwreck, and would have him say whether he did not now acknowledge the power of the gods, – "Aye," asked he again, "but where are they painted that were drowned after their vows?" And such is the way of all superstition, whether in astrology, dreams, omens, divine judgments, or the like; wherein men, having a delight in such vanities, mark the events where they are fulfilled, but where they fail, though this happen much oftener, neglect and pass them by."

The confirmation bias allows us to consolidate every sort of belief, even the most insignificant ones, like our superstitious fixations which can only be instilled into us because we make efforts to remember *only* the lucky incidents favored by one ritual or another, as the most remarkable. It is the confirmation bias which allowed an unpleasant case to develop in Seattle in the middle of the last century.

1.3. The Seattle affair

Around the end of the 1950s, a collective psychosis took over Seattle. In restaurants, on the street, at their workplace, etc., people only talked about one strange incident: a number of windshields were found to be pockmarked by little cracks. As the news spread around the city, everyone wanted to verify the condition of his or her car. The rumor grew bigger and soon became a point of concern on everyone's lips. Why had car windshields become like that?

This mystery momentarily drew the attention of public opinion and became such a big issue that President Eisenhower, at the state governor's request, saw fit to mobilize a team of experts in order to shed light on it. These investigators first realized that two competing convictions clashed with each other. According to the first theory, called "the fallout", people were dealing with the consequences of Soviet nuclear tests, which had polluted the atmosphere. The fallout resulting from this contamination, by means of a drizzle that was corrosive on glass, created this epidemic of cracked windshields.

The second theory, named "the asphalt", indicted the redevelopment of road networks issued by Governor Rosollini. This highway plan was thought to create a frequent spatter of acid drops generated by the new road surface, favored by the humid weather typical of Puget Sound.

The investigators, undoubtedly because they were not steeped in this atmosphere of belief, found these two explanations dubious. As a methodical way of thinking should work in such circumstances, they first tried to verify the facts. Was it really true that all windshields had been damaged? Then, they examined those cars carefully and actually noticed the presence of microfissures on the windshields, but they also realized that these little cracks were barely visible to the naked eye. What about the windshields in neighboring towns? By asking this simple question, they showed they were capable of freeing themselves from the confirmation bias. It was enough to drive some 10 km to test this conviction, which had spread around Seattle, but this time through *contradiction*: if something strange was really happening in this city, then cars in neighboring towns should not present similar features. They discovered that, simply enough, the cars of the other towns they went to showed the same symptoms as those in Seattle.

In fact, as the rumor started to spread around the city, its residents began doing what they evidently did not normally do: they started very closely examining the windshield of their cars, and thus could see that sometimes it was actually streaked with little crevices. However, as experts declared, this was nothing more than the natural, and generally unnoticed, consequence of the wear and tear of their car. Watzlawick [WAT 78, p. 81] was then right to remark about this case that: "What Seattle experienced was not an epidemic of pockmarked windshields, but an outbreak of examined ones".

If those living in Seattle, rather than verifying whether their windshield was actually pockmarked, thus *confirming* the belief, could have observed the windshields of the cars in neighboring towns, they would have realized that this conviction was *invalid*.

1.3.1. *The Wason experiment*

As was suggested by Bacon's remarks and illustrated by the Seattle affair, the approach of belief refutation is quite unintuitive for the ordinary man's mind. It is something that can be tested experimentally, as Wason did in 1966. The British psychologist introduced a four-card, ostensibly quite simple, game to some volunteers.

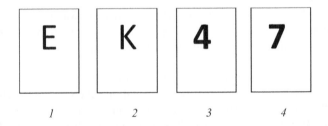

After the explanation that it is possible to find two letters on the front, **E** or **K** and, similarly, two figures on the back, **4** or **7**, this question is asked: "Which cards need to be turned over to verify the following statement: *if a card has a vowel on one side, it has an even number on the other?*"

The solution consists of turning over cards **1** and **4**, but the vast majority choose cards **1** and **3**. By doing this, we focus on the cases that *confirm* the rule, rather than on those that *contradict* it. It seems natural to think that *card* **3** confirms the rule set by the statement of the problem, which is the case if we find a vowel when we examine its back. However, we could find a consonant on it without this rule being broken. The only card (apart from the first card) able to establish its validity is the fourth card, since if it had a vowel on its back it would be evident that the statement is false.

This mental process offers a simple, yet significant, was of understanding the longevity of beliefs. We often notice facts which are not incompatible with a dubious statement, but this demonstration is of no value if we do not take into account the proportion, or even the existence, of those other facts that contradict it.

If this hankering for verification is not the expression of objective rationality, this somehow also makes life easier for us. Thus, the process of contradiction is undoubtedly more effective if our aim is to look for the truth, since it diminishes the probability of mistaking something false for true. However, it also requires a time commitment [FRI 93] that may, in the worst-case scenario, be deemed absurd, since it is then merely a matter of making a *satisfactory* decision. Drozda-Senkowska [DRO 97, p. 109] writes quite aptly about this: "Think about the multitude of decisions we take every moment. If we followed, for the most important ones, the contradiction approach what would happen? We would be permanently doubting and questioning everything. We would never take action".

Stoczkowski [STO 99] also humorously remarks that resorting to irreproachable reasoning procedures can be dangerous for our health. To rigorously test the notion that fire burns, should we not, he asks, make sure that it actually burns every part of our body? Maybe you have already burnt your hand by moving too close to the fireplace, which proves that fire can burn your hand, but have you already done the same with your foot? A contradiction approach would not accept to agree with the assumption that fire burns our body unless it could resort to a kind of method that common sense may legitimately regard as stupid and dangerous. Moreover, common sense is also supported on this point by Stoczkowski [STO 99 p. 393], who thinks it is obvious that sometimes "it is sensible not to be too rational, since there are circumstances where *efficient rationality* strangely resembles paranoia".

Fundamentally, social players accept certain objectively doubtful explanations because of their apparent *pertinence*, in the meaning Sperber and Wilson [SPE 89] gave to this term. In a situation of competition, they explain, we will opt for the proposition that produces the greatest cognitive effect with the least mental effort. The objectively right solution, when it exists, is often the most satisfactory as we experience when we find out the solution to a logical problem, but people do not always have enough imagination and motivation to conceive it and often surrender to what Fiske and Taylor [FIS 84] call our "cognitive avarice[3]". This often leads us to support doubtful, yet relatively convincing, beliefs since, when it comes to a number of subjects, we do not have enough motivation to become informed people. The fact is that if methodical knowledge often produces a cognitive effect superior to that of merely "satisfactory" propositions, i.e. beliefs, it also involves greater commitment. The probability of endorsing the former relies on how easily we find the latter.

About our mental avarice

To illustrate this idea, I suggest that you try to solve a little entertaining problem known in the published literature as the "*THOG Problem*" [WAS 77]. Here are the rules: we suppose that the experimenter has chosen two features that allow an object to be a "THOG": shape and color. There are only two possible shapes (heart and diamond) and two possible colors (black and gray). In order to be "THOG", an object only needs to possess *one* of the characteristics chosen by the experimenter (either color or shape), being a "not-THOG" when it has both or neither. We do not know what the experimenter's choice is, but we know that a black diamond is a "THOG". Consequently, are the black heart, the gray diamond and the gray heart "THOGS" or "not-THOGS"? It is possible to give three answers: such a figure is a thingie, it is not a thingie or it is impossible to determine whether it is one or not. This problem is summarized in the following table.

◆	♥	◆	♥
THOG	?	?	?

Three kinds of reasoning can be observed experimentally [ERI 83, EIR 89, O'BR 90]. The most common way of thinking is as follows: since the black diamond is a "THOG", the experimenter must have chosen either the diamond shape or the color black. Consequently, the gray heart, which possesses neither of these features, cannot be a "THOG". Similarly, the black

---

3 I showed experimentally [BRO 06, BRO 07a, BRO 07b] that, when faced with problems with an objective solution, people tend to regard this solution as superior to the others ... provided that they find it out, which does not happen too often.

heart and the gray diamond, which present one of these characteristics, are "THOGS". Thus, we obtain this result:

♦	♥	♦	♥
THOG	THOG	THOG	Non-THOG

Another kind of reasoning can be supported: the gray heart, which possesses neither of the characteristics that the black diamond does, cannot be a "THOG", but it is possible to deduce from the statement that the black heart and the gray diamond are. In fact, we do not know which characteristic was chosen by the experimenter. Now, if the color black was chosen, then the black heart is a "THOG", whereas the gray diamond is not. Reciprocally, if the diamond shape was chosen, then the gray diamond is a "THOG", whereas the black heart is not. Thus, we cannot find out whether the black heart and the gray diamond are "THOGS" or "not-THOGS", and we obtain the following result:

♦	♥	♦	♥
THOG	Insoluble	Insoluble	Non-THOG

These two lines of reasoning are chosen by most people due to their satisfactory appearance. They offer a solution to the question with a reasonable amount of mental commitment. They reveal our mental avarice *and* are completely false.

The only valid type of reasoning is the one chosen on average by only 10% of respondents. It is slightly beyond the scope of intuition and involves thus a greater commitment than other more immediate solutions. It can be formalized as such: since we know that the black diamond is a "THOG", we can deduce that the experimenter has chosen either the color black or the diamond shape as the "THOG" feature, but not both (since then the black diamond would not be a "THOG"). Hence, we can deduce that the gray heart is a "THOG". The black diamond is a "THOG" either because of its color, and consequently the second "THOG" characteristic must be the heart shape, or because of its shape, and the second "THOG" feature must then be the color gray. In either case, the gray heart corresponds to the definition of "THOG". However, neither the black heart nor the gray diamond can be "THOGs". In fact, if the "THOG" feature is the color black, its shape will have to be the heart. Consequently, the black heart will possess both features and the gray diamond neither. In either case, they are "not-THOGS". Reciprocally, if the "THOG" shape is the diamond, then its color will have to be gray. The black heart then does not present either of the "THOG" features, whereas the gray diamond possesses both. Consequently, the solution to the problem is as follows:

◆	♥	◆	♥
THOG	Non-THOG	Non-THOG	THOG

The solution to the problem formulated here is quite surprising and counterintuitive, but once we have discovered it, we *know* it is the right solution. The problem is that 90% of respondents to the experiment got misled by false solutions before reaching this conclusion. Their disorientation arises from the fact that their reasoning provides a solution to the problem (which is a strong incentive to stop thinking) and its erroneous nature is not immediately obvious. A great part of the problem derives from this very simple aspect of our mind's workings.

1.4. The theorem of information credulity

Since beliefs often propose solutions that suit our minds' natural inclinations, and since they rely on the confirmation bias, they will produce a cognitive effect beneficial to the mental effort involved. As Ross *et al.* [ROS 75] and Ross and Lepper [ROS 80] show, people, after accepting an idea, will persevere with their conviction. Their persistence will be all the more trouble-free since the increase in unselective dissemination of information has made it likelier for them to find "data" confirming their belief. I do not agree at all with the idea that the Internet biologically rewires our brain, as essayist Nicholas Carr affirms [CAR 08]. However, the fact that a mind looking for information on the Internet has to rely partially on the way a search engine organizes it seems acceptable to me. What the Web reveals is not a new way of thinking but, quite the opposite, one that is very old.

Does anyone trust in the efficacy of homeopathy? This person will find, due to any search engine on the Internet, hundreds of pages which allow him or her to strengthen his or her belief. We all know that, depending on our political orientation, we will tend to read a certain kind of newspaper more than others. It is easy to set the impression that we are wasting our time when we consult information sources that do not suit the way we see the world. Some social psychology research proves this fact. A study[4] carried out in 2006 and focused on the readers of political blogs unsurprisingly showed that 94% of the 23,000 respondents only read blogs that correspond to their leanings. Similarly, on Amazon, books on politics are bought more and more according to the buyers' political preferences. It is a fact as old as Man himself and the confirmation bias, and, taking into account the revolution of the cognitive market, it makes it possible to formulate the *theorem of information credulity*. This is based on the fact that the mechanisms of selective search for information are facilitated by the mass features that information now possesses. All of this helps to ensure the stability of the belief empire. This theorem can then be enunciated in its most simplified form as such[5].

The greater the amount of non-selected information within a social space, the more credulity will spread.

"Personally, to make sure, I check on the Internet"

On December 8th, 2011, I agreed to appear on a radio program that aired on Sud Radio, called "*Inquiry and investigation*", about conspiracy theories. The backdrop of this program was yet another development of the Dominique Strauss-Kahn affair. An American journalist, Edward Jay Epstein, claimed he could provide new elements, suggesting that the former managing director of the IMF might have been the victim of a conspiracy. To tell the truth, the conversation was less concerned with this matter than with the question of conspiracy in general. As it often happens, my participation in this kind of program resulted in a torrent of criticism.

"Gerald Bronner is exactly like one of those collaborators who want to deprive people of all of their judgments" is only one of the many criticisms found on a forum. However, this is not what struck me. One of my interlocutors, a fellow guest called Thomas, was quite in favor of a conspiracy-related view of reality and, in order to prove the solidity of his approach, he declared: "Personally, I verify every bit of information I come

---

4 http://www.themonkeycage.org/blogpaper.pdf.
5 Naturally, this theorem does not imply its converse.

across: when I hear "attack in Egypt" or elsewhere, I look it up on the Internet together with the word "conspiracy".

Thinking, of course, that he was expressing the impartiality of his point of view, Thomas provided unawares a perfect illustration of how the Internet could help the confirmation bias. Thomas, confident that he is employing an objective method to get his bearings in the information maze of the cognitive market, is unknowingly inoculating himself with a mental poison. I do not think that my arguments convinced him back then. However, today, it would be quite easy for him to become the subject of a little experiment and subsequently realize that I was right. Let us consider some current events important enough to have been commented about: the earthquake that hit Haiti in 2010 and Lady Diana's death. Let us suppose that Thomas employs his infallible method in order to "verify every piece of information". These are the results he would obtain:

	Lady Diana	Haiti earthquake
Without the word "conspiracy"	2	0
With the word "conspiracy"	20	15

Table 1.1. *Number of websites dedicated to conspiracy theories out of the first 30 results given by Google*

As regards the Diana affair, Thomas will have a 67% chance of being faced with conspiracy theories if he organizes his search around the terms "Diana" and "conspiracy". If he only looks up "Diana", his chance will be only 7%. As for the earthquake in Haiti, he has a 50% chance of finding conspiracy-related Websites, which drops to 0% if he deletes the word "conspiracy". This may seem obvious, but the fact remains that once Thomas had made this public claim he seemed to be confident he was displaying a form of intellectual rigor. He was doing nothing more than showing how much common sense may be deceived by the force of the confirmation bias. The cognitive market has become a sort of potluck dinner where we find as much as we bring; the fact is that the nature itself of Thomas's question was bound to lead him to what he wanted to find. At this stage, we may suppose that Thomas also ignored the existence of something else that further strengthens the expression of this confirmation bias once we resort to Google to get informed: *filter bubbles*.

1.5. Filter bubbles

Let us suppose that two different people, regular Internet users with dissimilar political, environmental and moral leanings, are looking up a piece of information on Google. They are not trying to find the address of the closest pizzeria, but data on death penalty, the financial crisis or the Arab revolutions. Are they going to be offered the same thing, and in the same order, by their search engine? No, if Eli Parisier [PAR 11] is right. Our searches on the Internet, especially if we use Google, are restricted by filter bubbles, which give us the information we asked for on the basis of 57 criteria, among which one our browsing history, our location, the kind of computer we own, our language, etc. This undoubtedly arises from the will to improve the performance of our searches: if someone living in Italy wishes to buy a piece of furniture, he or she will benefit from the fact the search engine will suggest shops located in Italy rather than Peru. However, this may become quite problematic if we want to steer clear of information that is already in line with our convictions, i.e. if we want to avoid being victim of the confirmation bias. If the search engine tends to display Websites according to an order that, we suppose, suits our inclination as consumer and citizen, then it is not only advertising banners that tend to confine us to a form of electronic expression of ourselves, but also, to an extent, information as it is shown on the first pages of Google.

Apart from Google, it seems that the organization of information on the Internet is resorting more and more to filter bubbles. So the *Washington Post*, owner of Slate.com, makes the use of Trove and *The New York Times* of News.me, two search engines that keep track of users' preferences to orient them toward information supposed to be of primary interest. Similarly, a piece of software called Findory allows the user himself/herself to program his or her preferred topics and subjects, but it reprograms itself if it appears that the user does not ultimately follow his or her own directions. We could multiply these examples by recalling, in particular, applications such as Flipboard and Zite, which can generate tablet-friendly magazines based on the users' social-networking feeds (Facebook and Twitter). Thus, people have a personalized mini-magazine. It is yet another aspect of the way technological progress sharpens an ancestral disposition of the human mind. This technological extension of our mental disposition can turn out to be quite useful for acts of day-to-day consumption or, indeed, if we prefer to be offered sports articles rather than pieces on social security management during our daily 30-minute commute. But, it may also be possible that it strengthens our comfortably preconceived, and not always truthful, ideas about the world.

Maybe the danger posed by filter bubbles is not as troubling, if we believe the "second inquiry" undertaken by Jacob Weisberg[6] on this matter. Do we find totally different things when we look up information, with the same keywords, on Google? Weisberg asked several people, whose leanings were quite dissimilar (someone working on Wall Street, a moderate democrat who manages a small to medium-sized business, a liberal and former programmer of the Slate Website, a transport worker with strong leftist tendencies, etc.), to use Google for keywords liable to be subjected to ideological fragmentation. It so happens that, with the support of screenshots, Weisberg did not find any significant difference between the results shown by the search engine. For Weisberg, Pariser's denunciation is mainly extremist and his fears unjustified[7]. When he took the initiative of questioning Google on this matter, he was told: "Actually we have algorithms that are specifically created to limit personalization and to promote variety on the results pages". Similarly, Jonathan Zittrain, law and informatics professor at Harvard, explains: "My experience makes me think that the effects of search personalization are minor". I have to say that the numerous experiences that I have conducted with my students about the relationship between beliefs and the Internet have led me to be less alarmist than Pariser on this point, but I will return to this. The phenomenon of filter bubbles does exist and provides further assistance to the expression of the confirmation bias on the modern cognitive market, but it is undoubtedly marginal for the time being. There are several much more important things than these filter bubbles concerning what controls the organization of the presentation of information on the Internet, as we will see now.

---

6 http://www.slate.fr/story/39977/web-bulle-personnalisation-google.
7 Pariser was the manager of the liberal activist group Moveon.org.

2

Why Does the Internet Side with Dubious Ideas?

2.1. The utopia of the knowledge society and the empire of beliefs

Like several major technological innovations, the Internet has roused many fears and hopes, and various well-selling books testify to both the former and the latter[1]. Some think that the Web, as it allows an exponential mass diffusion of information and *potentially* free access to this information for everyone, seems capable of giving rise to the *knowledge society*. This notion, first used by Drucker [DRU 69] and on several occasions taken up again and expanded on [MAN 98, STE 94], is based on one observation: the alterations of our production systems have led our societies to regard knowledge and innovation as key factors in economic development, and free access to this knowledge as the fundamental issue of our democratic future. The theory of the knowledge society claims to be analysis and political project at once. From this perspective, the UNESCO world report *Towards Knowledge Societies* may be regarded as a sort of manifesto (p.17): "The current spread of new technologies and the emergence of the Internet as a public network seem to be carving out fresh opportunities to widen this public knowledge forum. Might we now have the means to achieve equal and universal access to knowledge, and genuine sharing? This should be the cornerstone of true knowledge societies, which are a source of human and sustainable development."

---

1 See for example, Tapscott [TAS 08] about the hopes and Bauerlein [BAU 08] about the fears.

This report is fundamentally based on a two-point analysis: on the one hand it acknowledges the existence of a *digital divide*, i.e. the gap between and within societies themselves concerning access to information sources, contents and infrastructures. This digital divide has the potential to hinder the development of knowledge societies, and thus it is important to reduce it quickly, not only to favor democratic values, but also to boost economic development everywhere. On the other hand, it explains that this effort, if necessary, would not be adequate since (p. 47): "Transforming information into knowledge presupposes an effort of reflection. Information as such is only raw data, the basic material for generating knowledge." Thus, it is necessary to take note of the existence of a "cognitive fracture" that characterizes people's inequality (essentially because of the difference between education levels) in terms of the "mastery of certain cognitive, critical and theoretical skills that are precisely what knowledge societies will seek to develop". This mastery would allow a person, according to the authors of the report, to find his bearings in the sea of information, thus enabling him or her to find the dry land of knowledge.

The moral and political intentions of this program are quite likeable, but it is not mandatory to accept its analysis without discussion. The assessment provided by the UNESCO report – which claims the expertise of famous names: Régis Debray, Jacques Derrida, Jean-Pierre Dupuy, Françoise Héritier, Julia Kristeva, Bruno Latour, Jean d'Ormesson, Paul Ricœur, Dan Sperber, Alain Touraine and many others[2] – seems questionable if we take into account the mechanism of actual competition between knowledge and belief products[3]. I do not wish to discuss here, point by point, the program of the knowledge society. Instead, I choose merely to allude to it since, in my opinion, it reveals an error of judgment on the processes of non-selective dissemination of information that characterizes the relationship between cognitive supply and demand, especially on the Internet.

2.2. The ditherer's problem

We have seen that the ease with which information is accessed and mass-disseminated is advantageous to the confirmation bias, which is the cornerstone of any belief's longevity. But there is something else, which the

---

2 These authors cannot be held responsible for the arguments supported by the report, which, however, mentions them by acknowledging that it has "benefited from the [authors'] initial contributions and analyses".
3 Further on, I will discuss the possible demarcation between the two.

different critics of the Internet culture do not seem to have realized: the fact is that the cognitive market is hypersensitive to the structure of supply, and automatically to the providers' motivation. This is one of the main factors in the organization of cognitive competition on this market.

Information seeking can be carried out from two main perspectives. On the one hand, this search can be handled through the confirmation bias: we already have a belief (which may be conditional) and we will tend to look for information in order to reinforce it. This is often the case when we think, for example, about social networks. Whatever his point of view, a Facebook member "posts" a piece of information on his wall, whether it is supposed to be funny or shocking, his "friends" often react by carrying on the same wavelength by producing other related information and links, thus substantiating the idea the user started with. Naturally, there may be arguments on Facebook but when these different orientations are stubbornly carried on, friends soon separate and take refuge in a friendly niche that is more favorable to their ideas. Facebook itself is conceived in this sense, since it allows us to "like", but not to "dislike", a post.

On the other hand, this search can be carried out with no preconceived ideas and thus without the hovering danger posed by the confirmation bias. This may happen either because of our incompetence – "I would like to know a little bit more about Armenia, I have no knowledge about that country" – or because we have no definite ideas about the topic yet, i.e. we have some knowledge but we remain undecided – "I hear a lot of contrary opinions about nuclear energy and its dangers, I would love to know more".

This scenario depicts an *irresolute* person. It is crucial since there is reason to believe that, statistically, it is him/her who is likelier to be influenced by the structure of the cognitive market he/she will join. In other words, since he/she has not formed a definite idea on the topic, he/she is going to be more sensitive than anyone else to the way the cognitive market makes this or that kind of argument more accessible. It is as if a shopper wanted to buy a box of washing powder at a supermarket without having any specific ideas about the right brand for him. This person is likelier than others (who, when looking, will give priority to their usual brand) to be influenced by the shelf layout. I have tested this hypothesis by conducting, with some students, an experiment on how convictions change.

Experiment on changing convictions about near-death experiences in relation to Internet use

The aim of this experience[4] was to evaluate the possible influence of Internet use in relation to the belief in near death experiences (NDEs). What do they consist of? People claiming to have lived through a NDE often had a serious accident where they almost died. They recount that, upon losing consciousness, they saw a white tunnel or they simply floated over their own bodies. More or less all of us have heard of these accounts. The 103 subjects[5] of this experiment had all heard of NDEs and they were asked, after a brief discussion on the topic, to assess on a scale from 0 to 10 (0 meaning that they did not believe that at all and 10 that they were absolutely convinced), their belief in the notion that these phenomena revealed the existence of an afterlife. Afterwards, they were given access to a computer connected to the Internet and they were asked to spend 15 minutes researching this topic as they understood it, knowing that the search engine used, Google Chrome, could list every website visited and determine the time spent on it. Then, a second interview began in order to evaluate the way the subjects' feelings had changed, or remained the same, about this matter. Finally, to conclude the interview, they were asked again to assess their belief on a scale from 0 to 10. To analyze these results, I thought that scores between 0 and 2 *and* 8 and 10 expressed a strong conviction (that NDEs prove the existence of an afterlife, or the opposite). Reciprocally, a score between 3 and 7 indicated a more uncertain conviction. The general results show that 69 subjects do not change their mind while 34 do modify their point of view. The conditions of the experiment did not favor these changes because the allotted time was short (15 minutes) and, because some of the subjects were keen to show that they were not turncoats and had clearly defined ideas: they were loath to admit they could be influenced by the Internet. Despite these difficulties, these results reveal something interesting. If we analyze the difference between those who started with a strong conviction (47) and those who had a less defined point of view (56), we notice that most of those who changed their mind after searching the Internet belong to the latter group. As for the "convinced", only the 11% modify their point of view (even marginally), whereas the figure grows to 52% for the other group. Now, among the

---

4 I want to thank here the Strasbourg students who graduated in 2011/2012 for the intra-annual survey: without their material help this experiment would not have been possible.
5 They had been chosen according to their age and were equally divided into five categories: (18-30); (31-40); (41-50); (51-60); (60+).

"versatile", 26.5% affirm they deem it less likely that NDEs reveal the existence of an afterlife, whereas 73.5% strengthen their conviction.

In this experiment, not only did most of the "versatile" belong to the undecided group, but their versatility led them to a mystical, rather than rational, understanding of these phenomena. Is it any wonder? Not really if we pay close attention to the organization of the cognitive market around a certain number of topics or, to return to the supermarket metaphor, to the way shelving makes some products more available than others. This matter is crucial because, as we have just seen, it involves the undecided in search of information. What kinds of products will they be faced with? Can we get an idea of the nature of the competition that characterizes the coexistence, on this market, of clashing products?

2.3. Competition between belief and knowledge on the Internet

To find an answer to these questions the author examined what an Internet user with no preconceived ideas could be "offered" on many topics on the Web. To simulate his approach, he took into account the survey results[6] about people's cultural practices in the digital age, which unsurprisingly show that we search the Internet more and more. We can also notice that for people in the 15 to 24 year-old range, for the first time since the appearance of television, the time spent in front of the small screen (besides the time taken dedicated to newspapers, books and radio) has dropped whereas the time devoted to the Internet has not stopped increasing. This shows that information searching on the Internet represents a growing share of the young's *demand* on the cognitive market. We can also see that it is youth as a category that contains the largest proportion of people ready to believe what they read on forums or on social networks[7]. Furthermore, half of Internet users spend more than 70% of their time online looking for information on search engines, among whom Google has attained an oligopolistic position (nearly 49 billion searches were carried out on this search engine during July 2008, i.e. 65 million searches every hour) [POU 11, p. 59]. Besides an Internet user, whenever his or her search is unsuccessful, in 76.4% of cases the searcher will try a second time with a

---

6 This is drawn from Donnat [DON 08] and from the data available at http://docs.abondance.com/question14.html.
7 https://docs.google.com/viewerng/url=http://www.lejdd.fr/var/lejdd/storage/original/media/files/societe/sondage-opinionway-pour-luejf-les-propos-haineux-sur-internet-fevrier-2015-pdf.

different keyword *but* the searcher will keep using the same search engine, rather than trying a new one. This persuaded me to use Google to simulate how the average Internet user could gain access to a certain cognitive offer.

Google owes part of its popularity to some simple, yet clever, technical devices. The actual algorithms that organize the effectiveness of the world's first search engine remain secret, but we know that its cornerstone is called pagerank (PR). It is an algorithm that gauges the importance of a Website in relation to its popularity. This measurement is established mainly on the basis of the number of links to a Website, and this number itself is weighed depending on the popularity of the websites that originated these links. To establish this, thousands of robot programs roam all over the World Wide Web. Thus, the higher the "pagerank" of a website, the greater its chances of being clicked on. The *availability of supply* is thus somehow revealed by the workings of Internet itself.

The question I asked myself was very simple: what will an Internet user, who does not necessarily have any preconceived ideas, be offered on Google in relation to the five following topics: astrology, the Loch Ness Monster, aspartame (sometimes considered to be carcinogenic), crop circles and psychokinesis.

The experiment I have undertaken on these topics does not claim to settle the question of what an Internet user will find convincing or unconvincing among all the pieces of information presented to him or her by Google, even if it is well understood that the nature of the source as it is perceived by the user will play a part in the credibility of the information [BOV 53, CHA 08, SHE 61].

These topics have also been chosen because scientific orthodoxy disputes the veracity of the beliefs they give rise to. This happens with psychokinesis [LAU 80, BRO 89], the Loch Ness Monster, crop circles seen as marks left by extraterrestrials, astrology[8], and also with the suspicions once focused on

---

8 Astrology is a doctrine that, to my knowledge, no scientifically-oriented person would ever support. Not because of ideological aversion, but simply because the two hypotheses on which it is built, 1) *our personality is influenced, even determined, by the configuration of celestial objects at the time of our birth* and 2) *our destiny, our future, and the fate of the world in general are themselves influenced or determined by the evolution of these celestial positions*) have been invalidated by arguments that seem definitive. For the latest developments on the arguments generally accepted by the scientific community, see Lequèvre [LEQ 02].

aspartame[9]. These five topics represent an interesting vantage point from which to assess the balance of power, on the cognitive market, between the information deemed orthodox by the scientific community and the information that is instead rejected, which the author will consequently treat as beliefs[10]. The word "belief" is not used here to disqualify these propositions – there is no need now to examine the question of the veracity of these statements – but to underline a reality which would vanish without this distinction. In other terms, what needs examining here is the competition between two types of statements, both claiming to give an account of the same phenomena, but only one of which has the possibility of invoking the consensus of scientific expertise. It goes without saying that in no case are these propositions an expression of public opinion in general or, more specifically, of Internet users; however, they give an idea of the Internet's offer to meet information demand.

Search engines, however, often display hundreds, even thousands, of websites about any given topic and it is common knowledge that a user would never read through all of those to find information. Thus, to make my research more realistic, the author only focused on what we know about the users' behavior: 65% of them merely check the first page (the first 10 websites), 25% stop at the second page (the first 20 websites), and only 5–10% go on to the third page before concluding their search. More than 95% of Internet users go no further than the first 30 pages. Besides, 80% of them key in at most two keywords for their search.

The method they chose was always the same: among thousands of websites mentioned by the search engine, they only checked the first 30. Furthermore, they conducted his research by always using the shortest and most neutral input they could: "psychokinesis", "Loch Ness Monster",

---

9 i.e. the methyl ester of a dipeptide, which is a molecule constituted by the combination of two amino acids. It is a non-nutritive substance with a sugary taste 200 times stronger than sugar. This misgiving was roused by an Italian study – Soffriti *et al.* [SOF 06] – which claimed to have shown that the consumption of this substance could favor the development of cancerous tumors in rats. It so happened that this experiment was rejected as invalid by the scientific community and especially by European Food Safety Authority, since the bias in its procedure was so significant that it invalidated the results obtained [EFS 06].

10 The question of the relationship between belief and knowledge is complex. The author proposed [BRO 03] adaptable elements of demarcation between these cognitive objects.

"aspartame", "astrology", "crop circles"[11]. The first 30 websites displayed by Google on these topics were then put into four possible categories:

– *Irrelevant websites:* On the one hand, a website is considered irrelevant when its content uses a theme as a pretext to address a completely different topic, as does this website advertising lamps in the shape of the Loch Ness monster: http://www.gizmodo.fr/2010/03/11/le-monstre-du-loch-ness-nest-pas-en-ecosse-mais-dans-mon-salon.html (7th website displayed for the input "Loch Ness Monster"). On the other hand, it is considered irrelevant when its content does not develop any argument or point of view in relation to the belief we are interested in, as is the case for the forum of this website, dedicated to the discussion of the chemical formula of aspartame: http://forums.futura-sciences.com/chimie/223689-formule-aspartam.html (19th Website displayed for the input "aspartame").

– *"Neutral" websites:* A website is considered neutral when it deals with the opposite arguments of both scientific orthodox propositions and unempirical beliefs, regardless of its context (even when it is a website favorable to any other kind of conviction). For example the AMESSI website (11th result displayed for the input "aspartame"), which promotes aromatherapy as much as hypnotism, offers a seemingly impartial article about aspartame – reminding readers that the dangers posed by aspartame are not scientifically proven and yet constantly emphasizing that suspicions are alive and well – and it is thus classified as "neutral".

– *Websites against beliefs:* A website is considered skeptical either when it only develops arguments and points of view detrimental to beliefs, or when it only deals with the arguments supported by believers to better emphasize their futility.

– *Websites pro-beliefs:* A website is considered pro-belief either when it only develops arguments and points of view advantageous to beliefs, or when it only deals with the arguments supported by skeptical to better emphasize their futility.

---

11 This approach is pertinent to the extent that the results can supposedly be obtained by *any Internet user* on average. Filter bubbles must be taken into account since, if we believe Pariser [PAR 01], Google displays to every user a list of different websites depending on his or her leanings. We saw above (see section *The filter bubbles*) that their importance was certainly overestimated. I agree with this since, year after year, in his seminar on collective beliefs students attempt to test these findings and always get similar results to those I am going to show.

The following sections give the results obtained for the first 30 websites – displayed by Google and classified according to their orientation – on five heterogeneous objects of belief.

2.4. Psychokinesis

Psychokinesis is the alleged ability to exert mental influence on an object, a process, or a system without using known mechanisms or forms of energy. Websites in favor of the hypothesis that mind powers exist are the most numerous, followed by the neutral ones, and ultimately by the skeptical ones. They represent, if we only take into account websites that clearly take sides, 74% of the views expressed, against 26% in favor of the skeptics[12].

	In favor	Against	Neutral	Irrelevant
Psychokinesis	17 (74%)	6 (26%)	7	0

Table 2.1. *Orientation of the first 30 websites displayed by Google in relation to the topic of psychokinesis*

2.5. The Loch Ness Monster

The Loch Ness Monster topic alludes to the hypothesis that a creature, unknown to official zoology or at least considered to be extinct, lives in the waters of the Scottish lake.[13] This topic, as we can see, produces a large number of irrelevant websites (27%), which can be attributed to the legendary creature's fame, which inspires fictions and subjects relayed from certain websites but unrelated to the belief itself. Pro-belief websites are the most numerous, followed by the irrelevant ones. If we only take into account websites that clearly take sides, they represent 78% of the opinions expressed, against 22% in favor of the skeptics.

---

12 Research on this matter was conducted on 28/08/10 and on 23/08/10.
13 This study was conducted on 13/07/2010.

	In favor	Against	Neutral	Irrelevant
Loch Ness monster	14 (78%)	4 (22%)	4	8

Table 2.2. Orientation of the first 30 websites displayed by Google in relation to the topic of the Loch Ness Monster

2.6. Aspartame

One of the hypotheses about aspartame claims, in opposition to international scientific expertise, that this molecule poses dangers to our health. The author has chosen the keyword "aspartame", which seemed less biased to him than "aspartame and health" or "aspartame and cancer"[14]. The drawback of such a vague statement was its lack of discrimination, so that we find a significant number of "irrelevant" websites (23%) for this topic too. Once again, pro-belief websites are the most numerous, followed by irrelevant websites. If we only take into account websites that clearly take sides, they represent 70% of the opinions expressed against, 30% in favor of the skeptics, which makes it the weakest balance of power recorded. Given the smallness of the sample considered, we should still be cautious, but maybe is it because economic issues are at stake on this theme (at least for aspartame producers) and, in these circumstances, some skeptics may have more important reasons to express their point of view. We will come back to this.

	In favor	Against	Neutral	Irrelevant
Aspartame	14 (70%)	6 (30%)	3	7

Table 2.3. Orientation of the first 30 websites displayed by Google in relation to the topic of the health hazard posed by aspartame

2.7. Crop circles

Crop circles are large circles that mysteriously appear, in general, in wheat fields[15]. They can be simple circles or have more complex shapes. No one doubts that these incidents actually happen, but there are various clashing

---

14 This study was conducted on 15/07/2010.
15 This study was conducted on July 19th to 21st 2010. It laid claim to the creation of these "artworks". This does not dissuade some people from stating that those circles cannot all be hoaxes since, they say, some seem too complex and regular to be man-made overnight. They even mention the occurrence of biochemical events.

interpretations. The most immediate sees it as a hoax, particularly as these phenomena, which mainly happened in the south of England in the 1980s, could easily be reproduced artificially. Incidentally, in October 1991, two artists, Doug Bower and Dave Chorley, claimed that they had been the creators of more than 200 crop circles since 1976. All over the world, groups called *circle makers* follow these phenomena, which would then exclude the hoax and the artwork hypotheses. Then they allude to the notion that these circles may be created by the action of extraterrestrial technology. The theory according to which they may be alien landing strips is one of the most common and was popularized in Night Shyamalan's movie *Signs*. Pro-belief websites are the most numerous. If we only take into account websites that clearly take sides, they represent 87% of the opinions expressed, against 13% in favor of the skeptics. However, we note that this topic gathers the largest number of "neutral" websites. Even when data come from websites open to any kind of beliefs, moderate and cautious opinions are often expressed, as was the case with psychokinesis, maybe because both topics have given rise to notorious frauds.

	In favor	Against	Neutral	Irrelevant
Crop circles	14 (87%)	2 (13%)	12	2

Table 2.4. *Orientation of the first 30 websites displayed by Google in relation to the topic of crop circles.*

2.8. Astrology

The economic issues at stake for the theme of astrology undoubtedly justify why the balance of power is tilted so strongly in favor of belief for the first 30 websites displayed by the search engine[16].

	In favor	Against	Neutral	Irrelevant
Astrology	28 (97%)	1 (3%)	0	1

Table 2.5. *Orientation of the first 30 websites displayed by Google in relation to the topic of astrology*

So, if we only take into account websites that clearly take sides, we can see that 97% of them are in favor of astrology. In general terms, the

---

16 The study about astrology was conducted on 12/07/10.

economic factor, which should not be ignored, still cannot explain how the balance of power is *always* unfavorable to orthodox knowledge for the five topics analyzed, even when no evident interests are at stake.

2.9. Overview of results

If we average out the results obtained for these five topics, we find out that, out of the websites that clearly take sides, 81.2% are pro-belief. This kind of result is confirmed year after year by students, who carry out the same experiment with similar themes: the lunar effect on births, the existence of Lizardmen, telepathy and various conspiracy theories. These results seem as achievable in the French-speaking world as they do in the English-speaking world, or even in the Chinese one – at least in relation to the "crystal skulls" myth (these alleged Mesoamerican sculptures are regarded by some as supernatural in origin and power), the only topic on which one Chinese student focused (he has to confess that he has not checked his results because of my linguistic incompetence, so he can vouch for their exactitude on a *trust* basis).

2.10. How can we explain these results?

The Internet reveals some very distinctive interactions between pieces of information. In particular, the structure of supply depends much more, for certain subjects, on the suppliers' motivation than it does on the buyers', and it especially relies on those who are technically able to create competitive and contradictory offers. In other terms, believers are generally *keener* than skeptics to support their point of view and to devote time to it.

The first reason is that conviction plays a major role in the believer's identity, who will easily be keen to look for new information that can make it more widely accepted. A conspiracy theorist, for example, will try to recall some of the arguments that make us believe that the 9/11 attacks were fomented by the CIA. A skeptic will often be indifferent. He/she will reject the belief, but he/she will need no reason other than the fragility of the statement he/she is dismissing. This can be seen on forums. Out of the 23 forums examined for all the topics combined, nine cannot be used because of their "irrelevance". Across the remaining 14, 211 points of view are expressed: 83 pro-belief, 45 against and 83 neutral. Upon reading the forums, what is striking is that skeptics often merely write ironic messages, making fun of conviction rather than developing an argument against it, whereas those who support a statement bring up arguments in favor of it, despite their unevenness (links, videos, copied and pasted sections of text, etc.). Out of the posts written by those who support a belief, 36% are backed by text, a link, or a developed argument, which is the case for only 10% of the skeptics' posts.

The second reason is that those who can put forward a cogent list of arguments against the believers' claim are not too interested in doing so. Let us return to the astrology example. Any astronomer could easily promote some of the reasons that lead us to find astrological propositions dubious, which some actually do. However, most of the time they feel merely irritated by astrological claims since they pose no danger for them, and to fight them would be both time-consuming and of no institutional interest whatsoever. This is the position adopted in 1869 by Thomas Henry Huxley, the eldest Victorian scientist, with regard to spiritualism: "I have no time for such an inquiry, which would involve much trouble and much annoyance. The only case of spiritualism I have had the opportunity of examining into for myself, was as gross as imposture as ever came under my notice". Similarly, we could give an account of an astronomer's feelings toward UFOs: "I refuse to be questioned about this patent absurdity. I think the topic is dull through and through and serious scientists should not be involved with it unless they have nothing better to do (…) to devote a significant part of one's time to UFOs would be a professional suicide"[17].

We can understand these scientists' reasons, but their lack of motivation has resulted in believers, much more resolute than them, managing to institute a paradoxical cognitive oligopoly. Their point of view is much easier to find on the Internet than that of people who could effortlessly show the futility of astrological propositions. If this was already common knowledge in relation to the book market, the Internet has amplified the phenomenon to the extent that it considerably reduces the supply costs.

2.11. The Titanic syndrome

The author would like to recall in some detail a TV debate that took place on the French Channel 5 on 22nd April 1988 in order to illustrate the idea that sometimes it takes a lot of motivation to counter the believers' claims. This TV channel had started broadcasting regular brief confrontations at lunchtime. It was quite common for these to see scientists pitted against followers of the conventionally so-called pseudo sciences (astrology, etc.).

---

17 These two quotes are drawn from Renard ([REN 11], pp. 50–51).

Now, upon rereading *in extenso* the content of these debates [CUN 88], one is struck by how scientists rarely come across as actually convincing. There is a lingering feeling of support toward the pseudo sciences, often conveyed by such statements as: "I do not really believe in that, but there may be something true" or "There must be a grain of truth in it".

On that day, the debate saw Yves Galifret, psychology professor at the University of Paris VI, pitted against a "magician" called Desuart (a clairvoyant). The latter defended the existence of precognition and, in order to convince his audience, cited the history of Morgan Robertson's novel *Futility*, published in 1898, which describes "the greatest ocean liner ever built". Here is what Desuart stated: "1898. An American sci-fi writer, Morgan Robertson, writes a novel in which he talks about a massive ship that sets out on its maiden voyage on an April night. It carries 3,000 passengers, it is 800 feet long, it has a tonnage of 70,000 tons and, unluckily, it collides with an iceberg, it sinks and, since there are only 24 lifeboats, more than 1,000 people drown. This novel is real: 1898! Would you like to know what that fictional ship is called? The *Titan*. Now, in 1912 – 14 years later – the *Titanic* sinks on an April night after colliding with an iceberg. It was sailing at 25 knots per hour, it was 800 feet long, had a tonnage of 66,000 tons, and 1,000 people died because there were only 20 lifeboats." His interlocutor, Yves Galifret, is uncomfortable before the "evidence" presented live by Desuart and tentatively says: "First of all, your information needs to be verified scientifically...", then he adds: "coincidences do exist". The psychologist is certainly right but it is not clear whether his arguments have convinced the audience. The problem is that Yves Galifret is not prepared to counter a classical account of "parapsychologic" reasoning since, if a counterargument can be used, as we are going to see, it also entails a significant commitment in terms of time and mental energy, i.e. *motivation*. First of all it would have been necessary to read Robertson's novel, which the psychologist did not do (without a doubt he did not even know about its existence), but for that matter neither did Desuart, otherwise he would not have distorted its fiction as much as he actually did. So, he claims that the *Titan* was as long as the *Titanic*, which is not the case since, in the novel, the ocean liner measures 214 meters long against the actual 269 meters. This is a 55 meters difference, which amounts to nearly 30% of the *Titan*'s size. This difference may be marginal but it does play a certain role when we take into account how Robertson wrote his book, as we are going to see. Desuart is also mistaken, if not as much, about the ship's tonnage. Now we only have to consider the number of dead people and lifeboats. As for the former, the magician does not pay too much attention to details: he claims that "more than 1,000 people die" on the *Titan* and 1,000 on the *Titanic*. It is this vagueness in his formulation that leads us to believe that the figures mentioned in Robertson's novel are prophetic. Actually, the number of victims in the novel amounts to 2,897, whereas the actual fatalities were 1,523, which still constitutes a difference of close to 100%. As for the lifeboats, it is true that, in both cases, there were not enough.

These preliminary remarks will most certainly fail to convince someone who wants to believe that Robertson's novel was somewhat prophetic. The believer will not be convinced by these details, since he or she will still be persuaded that this is a fictional tale that foresees, broadly speaking and with relative accuracy in its details, a tragedy that will occur 14 years later. Would it not be hypocritical to deny this?

Morgan Robertson was quite knowledgeable about the maritime world, being the son of a captain; he was a cabin boy for around 10 years on freighters. In short, he was a writer specialized in maritime adventures. It would not be crazy then to imagine that he was keeping himself up to date about the latest developments in shipbuilding. The building of enormous liners was quite rightly on everyone's lips even before Robertson had started writing his novel. It is thus unlikely that he did not know anything about the building of one of the biggest liners in the world, the *Gigantic*. It is all the more improbable since on September 16th, 1892, i.e. 6 years before the prophetic novel was published, the *New York Times* mentions the event: "The White Star shipping company has commissioned the prominent shipwright Harland and Wolf of Belfast to build a transatlantic liner that will break every size and speed record. The ship has already been named *Gigantic*: it will measure 700 feet long, 65 feet 7 and a half inches wide, and will make 45,000 horsepower. It is predicted to reach a cruising speed of 22 knots and a top speed of 27 knots. Moreover, it will be equipped with three propellers, two of which will be arranged like those of the *Majestic* and the third of which will be positioned at the center. This ship should be ready by the 1st of March 1894"[18]. Robertson undoubtedly draws from the *Gigantic* – which itself hoped to outshine the *Majestic* – for his *Titan* in terms of engine power, number of propellers or even dimensions. The characteristics of the *Titan*, which seem extraordinarily similar to those of the *Titanic* to the ordinary person, are actually automatically linked to the dimensions of the liner. So,

_____

18 This quote is drawn from Bélanger [BEL 99].

the number of watertight compartments cannot vary that much and the number of lifeboats was, at that time, linked to the ship tonnage. As their number did not depend on the number of passengers, there was bound to be a shortage of lifeboats, a fact of which Robertson was well aware and from which he undoubtedly drew his inspiration as a writer. It is after the *Titanic* tragedy that things changed. In other words, once a ship tonnage has been established, a certain number of elements (number of watertight cabins, speed, engine power, number of lifeboats, etc.) must depend on it and subsequently the prophetic qualities of *Futility* become much less interesting. Robertson did nothing more than follow the competition between shipbuilders and write a well-informed futuristic novel. Many novels revolving around the sea were written back then, thus it is not surprising that one of them anticipated the tragic incident. Do we recall that both the *Titan* and the *Titanic* sank in April? Once again, if Robertson wants to relate the story of a liner, deemed unsinkable, that defies the forces of nature, he needs to find a plausible cause for its shipwreck. Given the size of the ship, an iceberg is an ideal candidate. Robertson knows, as the sea connoisseur he is, that this is one of the greatest dangers for a ship of those dimensions. He also knows that this danger is particularly real in April, a period of snowmelt.

We cannot bear our colleague Galifret a grudge for not having been ready to reply appropriately to all the lines of argument put forward by a believer. The problem underlined by this example is a common problem. Scientists in general have no interest, whether academic or personal, in devoting time to this competition. It is understandable, and yet this situation quite paradoxically results in believers having managed to institute a cognitive oligopoly across a wide spectrum of subjects both on the Internet and in the official media, which have become fairly sensitive to the sources of heterodox information across a range of themes.

2.12. When Olson's paradox plays against knowledge

The existence of this cognitive oligopoly illustrates Olson's famous paradox [OLS 78]. What is it about? Let us suppose that five people share the same interests. By joining forces they could profit, let us say, in economic terms. However, everyone knows that in order to make a profit it is necessary to invest some time and money. Their possible gain would far exceed this investment, but they are also well aware that there is no need for all of them to make this commitment. It is only necessary for some of them to commit since, if they are successful, everyone will benefit. Olson's paradox may occur when it is in the general interest, with everything to gain, to act collectively, which does not actually happen since many expect to profit from a collective claim without having to pay their share (in terms of time, energy or even money). It is the "let someone else do it" strategy. Since it is in someone's best interests to let others do the work and thus profit from a very advantageous gain/cost ratio, it is inevitable that many refrain from acting and this collectively attractive objective cannot be met. These kinds of paradoxical situations are always favorable to those groups; however, small a minority they might be, they are keen to impose their point of view. These small groups can thus dominate larger groups, since the members of the latter, as irritated, stunned and dismayed as they may be by the stance of the former, are never keen enough to disagree and take over the market of cognitive supply. Thus, orthodox knowledge is paradoxically outvoted on many topics. The "rationalistic" world is an exception to this tendency since its members, on account of their militancy, are sufficiently eager to devote time and mental energy to this opposition. Out of all the opinions against the five beliefs whose presence on the Internet the author examined, 37% belong to self-styled rationalistic websites (the Art of Doubt, AFIS, the "Sceptiques du Québec"…). If we exclude the aspartame case, where skepticism was not particularly pronounced, the figure goes up to 54%.

The fact that the Internet is a cognitive market hypersensitive to the structure of supply and to the eagerness of suppliers is relevant way beyond the boundaries of the topic of "conviction" since, as Keen [KEE 07] remarked about Digg.com[19] – a website boasting 900,000 subscribers – 30 people were enough to determine a third of the texts displayed on the homepage. On Netscape.com[20], one user was the sole author of 217 published articles, i.e. 13% of all the most popular articles at the time. We can notice the same kinds of phenomena in relation to the online encyclopedia Wikipedia, since the 100 most active contributors have written more than a quarter of [FIL 10, p. 69]! This is a power law called 1/10/100, as Cardon explains ([CAR 10, p. 19]): "Whereas in real life every work team struggles to accept the unequal participation of its members, online voluntary cooperation is characterized by a great heterogeneity of commitments. The participation (…) of a tiny fraction of contributors is very active, so that a minority contributes regularly and everyone benefits from the community's resources without playing a decisive part in it."

---

19 Digg.com is a social news website where users choose their preferred articles and websites.
20 Netscape.com was a news website before being replaced by AOL.

The author finds it acceptable to suppose that this competition on the cognitive market draws from the believers' motivation, which is superior to the skeptics'. In other words, the believers are statistically more active than the skeptics. When there is a heated social debate on a topic, the skeptics are perfectly able to go into action and take their space, as is natural, in the public debate, but most of the time it is as if the soft underbelly of our contemporary rationalism were more and more, if paradoxically, giving way to irrationalism. If by "irrationalism" we mean "the organized discourse of contestation" over the ability of rationalist verification – as it has expressed itself in both theory and practice in the history of science – to generate and back statements whose descriptive and explicative power, *ceteris paribus*, is much superior to that of any other statement with the same ambitions – whatever its mental approach – then this irrationalism is truly wide-ranging. As I have already said, we would be very mistaken if he believed that, for me, this contemporary irrationalism, which counters scientific orthodoxy both bizarrely (crop circles, astrology, etc.) and more seriously (GMOs, waves and vaccines), has no reason to do what it does. Those who claim the right to doubt, and rightly regard it as a democratic principle, do not surrender to conviction without good reason. Not only do the new conditions of the cognitive market facilitate in part the propagation of this irrationalism, but they also strengthen its expressions, as diverse as they might be. The fact is that a cognitive product, in order to spread, needs to be *believed* and, since our contemporaries are not brainless, it also needs a solid argumentative system able to counter rationalistic arguments. This is what Charles Fort knew back in his time. If people did not pay attention to him back then, they certainly do now.

2.13. Charles Fort, his life, and his works in a few words

In 1910, Charles Fort resolved to take over and even go beyond the boundaries of scientific knowledge available in his time. This ambition may seem bizarre, but the man was the farthest thing from crazy. He allowed himself 8 years to excel in *every* science. It was a huge project; Charles Fort was indeed an eccentric. He was born in Albany in 1874 and died in New York in 1932, after jotting down four works that may easily be the strangest things ever written. He spent his life examining all sorts of facts, be they weird or serious (raining frogs, meteorites, allegedly inexplicable cataclysms, disappearances, etc.), which he named the "sanitarium for overworked coincidences".

Would Charles Fort remain a simple collector? Of course not. His ambitions were much higher: he wanted to believe that the world and all those strange facts that, according to him, eluded the knowledge of his time were evidence of the existence of hidden realities, which he planned to uncover. He may have supported untenable theories, such as the one that the Earth is flat, but he was neither crazy nor stupid and, if anything, most of his contemporaries attributed a form of atypical intelligence to him. His main passion was supporting improbable theories by backing them up with a large and heterogeneous number of arguments. Undoubtedly, he aimed to weaken the notions of argumentation and evidence themselves, his objective being a sort of knowledge by contradiction. In this sense, we can say that he was a strange and forgotten precursor of relativism. His first published work, and the most famous, is *The Book of the Damned*, which caused quite a stir upon its publication because of the incongruity of the theories he supported and was qualified by T. Winterich as "a *Golden Bough* for lunatics". What we have to focus on here is the method advocated by Fort to make conviction prevail. He described this method very metaphorically in the preamble to his book (FOR 55, pp. 23–24): "Battalions of the accursed, captained by pallid data that I have exhumed, will march. Some of them livid and some of them fiery and some of them rotten. Some of them are corpses, skeletons, mummies, twitching, tottering, animated by companions that have been damned alive. There are giants that will walk by, though sound asleep. There are things that are theorems and things that are rags: they'll go by like Euclid arm in arm with the spirit of anarchy. (...) The spirit of the whole is processional. The power that has said to all these things that they are damned is Dogmatic Science. But they'll march. (...) The solidity of the procession as a whole [will come from] the impressiveness of things that pass and pass and pass, and keep on and keep on and keep on coming".

In other words, Fort aimed to create an argumentative "*mille feuilles*": each layer of his demonstration might well have been fragile, as he confesses in the quoted passage, but the building will be so tall that the overall impression will be one of truthfulness. The equivalent of an expression like: "There must be a grain of truth in it."

It is undoubtedly necessary to have a glance at one of Fort's books to realize how he carries out his program but, to be honest, many 20th Century works, some of which have met with immense public acclaim, can be qualified as "Fortian" to the extent that they all at once mobilize arguments drawn from archeology, quantum physics, sociology, anthropology, history, etc. In most cases, these disciplines are mentioned quite casually, but their reference makes it possible to set up a line of argument that appears credible to the ordinary layman, who will be struck by such universal culture and will be neither competent nor keen enough to search, point by point, for the technical information that would quell the attraction these beliefs are going to exert on him or her. Each of these arguments, when taken separately, is actually quite weak but their sum seems as convincing as any body of evidence can be. This is what makes "Fortian" products appealing on the cognitive market: it is arduous to counter each of the arguments one by one since they make use of a number of competences too large for one person. Thus, someone will always be left with a feeling of ambiguity when unprepared as he or she is faced with these kinds of beliefs even without necessarily adhering to them. This is the best definition of what we may call a *Fort effect*, which is what Charles Fort unequivocally relied upon when he was writing *The Book of the Damned.*

2.14. Fort products: argumentative mille-feuilles

Jacques Bergier, who co-authored *The Morning of the Magicians* – one of the best-selling books of the 20th Century – with Louis Pauwels in 1960, claimed Fort's legacy and the right to argumentative eccentricity. One of the theories supported in this famous book is better known as the myth of the Ancient Astronauts [STO 99]. It claims that humankind was created by extraterrestrials and that a kind of initial knowledge, now forgotten, allowed our ancestors and their alien allies to build buildings (the Great Pyramid of Giza, Thihuanaco, etc.) that require sophisticated technological means. According to this myth, religions are nothing more than the muddled and incomplete transcript of the recollection of these events and the Gods mentioned by the sacred texts correspond to our distant space fathers. Several books have supported this kind of theory, among which are Robert Charroux's *One Hundred Thousand Years of Man's Unknown History* (1963) and especially Erich von Däniken's *Chariots of the Gods? Unsolved Mysteries of the Past* (which sold more than 40 million copies worldwide). The latter provided, to back up his theory, 80 "pieces of evidence", all heterogeneous, exclusively in relation to archeology or history: 44 archeological monuments, 12 Ancient Testament passages, three works written by the Essenes sect, 16 mystical accounts taken from non-Western cultures and five historical documents.

This proliferation of arguments made it possible to adopt a double line of defense. On the one hand, when some agreed to devote time to the technical discussion of the Ancient Astronauts myth [GAL 65], the supporters of these beliefs had no trouble rejecting facts, as Stoczkowski ([STO 99, p. 57]) states: "Did archeologists suggest recent dates? The argument would be hindered by questioning the reliability of the dating methods. Did they show evidence of primitive tools on megalithic statues? They would be told that savages had simply tried to work with their ridiculous axes on stones that had been previously laser-cut by aliens. Even the most irrefutable claims of fraud were unsuccessful. Of course there are counterfeit carved stones in Ica, Charroux and Von Däniken acknowledge at once, but out of thousands of forgeries there must be some authentic stones; why couldn't they be those on which dinosaurs or surgical procedures are represented?".

On the other hand, the supporters of the Ancient Astronauts myth all agreed, in the footsteps of Charles Fort, who inspired them, to admit that many of the elements backing this theory were mere conjectures. Bergier and Pauwels even claimed in advance that hundreds of them would undoubtedly turn out to be completely incoherent. However, taking up a line of reasoning we very often see, they add that "there must be a grain of truth in it". Consequently, one of their strategies revolved around the claim that, even if some of their arguments were proved to be false, this demonstration could not invalidate their theory given the sheer number of facts it was based on.

This *argumentative mille-feuilles* increasingly often characterizes the adulterated products that can be traded on the contemporary cognitive market. The success of a novel like *The Da Vinci Code* and the confusion it provoked in some minds are the direct consequences of a demonstration based on elements which are false, yet plausible to the ordinary layman, and numerous enough to create a Fort effect. This account, however fictional it may be, drew from essays that had already met with a certain public success for example [BAL 82] and that claimed to support factual theories.

In a similar way, contemporary conspiracy theories have been able to capitalize on this Fort effect to increase the base of their audience. Upon reading, even superficially, conspiracy websites, whether they attempt to shed light on the 9/11 attacks or on Michael Jackson's death, we are struck by the breadth of argumentation and by the hardships an unprepared mind has to go through in order to give a rational reply to this mass of pseudo evidence. The fact is that if Fort products have been around for a long time (at least since the start of the 20th Century), they have now taken over the public space due to the technical possibilities provided by the Internet.

2.15. The sharing of the arguments of conviction

Rumors and conspiracy theories have long been under the influence of the "utterance". These stories were spread around the social space by word of mouth and, while this still happens quite often, the Internet has provided them with a new means of expression. If formerly it was quite expensive to gain access to this market (to publish a book, to write an article on those media that reach a wide audience, etc.), this tool now allows everyone to produce a line of argument easily accessible by all (as a text, an image, a movie, etc.). This phenomenon entails three major things for the universe of belief. First of all, it makes it possible to reduce the volatility of every utterance, which is precisely what characterizes the exchange of information between people, as it was shown by Allport and Postman's famous works on rumor [ALL 47].

The first experiments on rumor

It was during WWII that people realized how rumor could actually be used as a weapon of war. This conflict underlined how propaganda could be devastating, employed for example to poison the mind of the enemy or to demoralize troops. The Office of War Information in particular took this matter very seriously and focused on it. It is in this light that we have to interpret Allport and Postman's works. These two authors, keen on unearthing some of the mechanisms of rumor diffusion, set up an experiment. It consisted of showing someone a picture or a drawing for 20 seconds. Afterwards, this person was asked to tell someone else what he or she had seen, without being allowed to see the picture in question. The second subject would then tell a third and so on, forming thus a chain of seven or eight witnesses. Now, the results of this experiment are spectacular. The descriptions given by the eighth subject generally have nothing to do with the actual content of the picture. These experiments provide a lot of information and underscore how our cultural system is characterized by the existence of underlying interpretations that will cause one image rather than another to come up with a certain probability. For example, one of the pictures showed a subway car in which a black man was sitting beside a white one, the latter holding a razor in his hands. The experiment showed that even after a few witnesses, the accounts described a threatening black man holding a razor in a subway car, probably about to assault a white man beside him. This reversal of the situation shows how likely this experiment on the ambiguity of communication was to bring to the foreground a stereotypical interpretation of a vague scenario. It uncovers the features of a biased system of information processing which, sometimes distorting cognition, is liable to promote beliefs.

Then, the stability that the written text gives to the account automatically entails an increased chance of memorization. The availability of information acts as a sort of mnemonic aid for people. Last, and most important for my intentions, this availability and this permanence of information enable cumulative processes, i.e. *a sharing of the arguments of belief*.

To tell the truth, it is not the Internet that allows these belief phenomena to monopolize these processes of information sharing. These may be somewhat useful when, for example, it is a matter of gathering scattered data about rare diseases [LOR 03]. Except that it is these mechanisms themselves that favor the accumulation of knowledge and contribute to the creation of "Fortian" cognitive products.

The disappearance of Malaysian Airlines flight MH370 thereby gave rise, via this deregulated information market, to morbid globalized speculation: pilot suicide, terrorist attack, alien abduction or even the evil actions of some elves – according to a shaman that we rightly allowed to have a say – etc. The number of speculators explains in part the staggering amount of hypotheses that were put forward and disseminated as quickly as only the Internet would ever make possible. This affair also reveals how the availability of information can excite our imagination and how fond our mind is of stories based on the portrayal of anomalies. So, was it not remarked that two people were traveling on fake passports? This element served as the basis for terrorist-related hypotheses, especially the one claiming that the plane had been hidden in a hangar for a "9/11" kind of attack. Was it not remarked that four people had not checked in for their flight? Only someone who has never taken a plane could find this surprising but, in the heat of the moment and in the torrent of comments we saw, any event can become a stepping stone to fiction. As more elements accumulated, the imagination grew so ramified that one of the hypotheses consisted of the notion that the whole tragedy was nothing more than a publicity stunt for the new season of *Lost*.

This whole affair can make us think some more about the difficulties posed by collaborative work, which by now accompanies every occurrence on the Internet. Thus well-intentioned Internet users all over the world tried to locate the plane debris with the help of a website called Digital Globe. Millions of different areas were regarded as the potential crash site, while this evidence was actually unusable. However, if an Internet user had found the debris by chance and if his or her evidence had not been used, people would have quickly started wondering: why have they concealed this discovery? Collective understanding, an inexhaustible Sisyphus, would have found several answers, not necessarily reassuring, and added yet another input to the mental sieve that our relationship with reality has now become. A sieve where truth and the illusion of truth are quite inextricably combined.

Up to this revolution of the cognitive market, conspiracy theories, when they did not lead to the publication of a book, preserved a relatively casual nature, could only pivot around some arguments that believers were able to memorize, and consequently had something outlandish about them. They could rarely meet one of the main criteria necessary to their success on the cognitive market: the credibility principle[21]. For example Marlboro, the cigarette brand, was accused of being under the heel of the Ku Klux Klan [CAM 02, p. 369]. The only evidence was that whenever we look at these cigarette packs in a certain way, they seem to be marked by three red Ks on a white background. These three Ks should be a proof of the influence exerted by the racist movement on Marlboro. It must be admitted that this argument is too weak to ensure that this curious proposition will be substantially and unconditionally circulated (unless it is a kind of ironic or anecdotic dissemination).

2.16. A Fortean product in the making: Michael Jackson's fake death

Nowadays a variation like: "they are hiding the truth" on such a classic theme as the death of a celebrity organizes a series of very sound arguments with a promptness ascribable to the possibilities of data sharing on the Internet. For example after Michael Jackson's death, the rumor that he was actually alive started circulating.

Some suspected that the staging of his own death would allow the singer, whose career was in decline, to come back triumphally. Those fans who refused to believe that the "King of Pop" had died dissected thousands of available documents and, as the old saying goes – "seek and ye shall find" –

---

21 Three factors play a major role in increasing the impact force of a cognitive product (independently from the characteristics of both the sender and the recipient of the message): the evocation factor, the credibility criterion and the memorization factor. See Bronner [BRO 06].

they managed to share some microelements that, once combined, formed a cognitive product more solid than people would think.

They underline that, first of all, Michael Jackson had seemed in good shape the last few times he appeared on television and nothing suggested he might soon have a heart attack. Besides this, the phone call to 911 came from a hotel 3 minutes from the singer's mansion, rather than from his own house.

Second, the self-styled *believers* wonder why he was given cardiac massage, which is only effective when performed on hard surfaces – as the cardiologist must have known – on his bed.

Third, the ambulance left the house in a clumsy and questionable way, reversing out on the main driveway where those paparazzi that will give this news to the world were standing.

Fourth, the pictures of the "King of Pop" being carried away show someone who looks much younger. They must be touched up: it is actually a picture taken a few years back when the singer was resting in his oxygen chamber. It is then discovered that the photographer who took these pictures was one of the singer's friends.

Fifth, a man no one knew, in a hat that partially covered his face, is present at the tribute ceremony and at the funeral service. The staff in charge of the ceremony is made up of dancers of the *This Is It* show the singer was working on. Now, strangely they are all smiling, as if they actually knew the truth.

In the sixth place, the recording of the funeral service is directed by Kenny Ortega into a sort of grandiose public display and the images broadcast are different from those shown by journalists.

We may also add the way *believers* interpreted the funeral message issued by the Jacksons or the picture (on the booklets received by those who had purchased a ticket for the concert which would never take place) where the King of Pop posed smiling behind a camera, or even his movements on the stretcher on the way to the hospital when he had already been given up for dead, etc. All of this makes some fans think that the whole incident was staged.

These processes of evidence accumulation are particularly useful for the conspiracy theorist's imagination since, unlike other conviction systems which are based on evidence or "facts", it is often enough for the conspiracy myth to unearth anomalies or enigmatic elements to generate an uncomfortable emptiness, which it soon fills up with a story. This account will be based on a *revelatory effect* or, in other terms, it will attempt to create a coherence out of the intriguing elements that until now seemed unrelated. This revelatory effect, as is the case when we eventually find the solution to a logic or mathematical riddle, provokes intense cognitive satisfaction, which dangerously inspires a feeling of certitude.

2.17. When Fort reinforces Olson

The Internet provides technical support to all of those who desire to combine argumentative elements which, when taken separately, may seem insignificant and easily invalidated but, when shared, create an argumentative corpus that requires those people who are trying to contradict it to spend time and energy. Things are much worse in relation to conspiracy theories that involve more important social issues, such as those about 9/11. This theory is supported by nearly a hundred different arguments! Some pertain to material physics, some others to seismology and others again to stock market analysis [ANF 10]. A counterargument would require competences that no man on his own can have. So, to mention only one argument out of the mixture, conspiracy theorists claim that the Twin Towers could not have collapsed the way they did, since they were held up by metal structures whose melting point was 2,800°F (i.e. 1,538°C). As David Heller explains, skyscrapers with metal structures have never collapsed just because of a fire [HEL 05]. Those of the World Trade Center should have been no exception since no kind of fuel, not even jet fuel, which is made of refined kerosene, can produce a temperature exceeding 1,500°F (i.e 816°C). The idea supported by the theorists, and also backed up by other technical arguments, claims that these buildings collapsed because they were blown up with dynamite, which is evidence that these tragic events had been planned by American policymakers who wanted them to pass off as spectacular terrorist attacks. This single argument is already disconcerting enough for anyone without knowledge about material physics: we can see then how a certain number of arguments, seemingly technical and yet easily understandable, may create a very appealing myth.

However, every argument put forward by conspiracy theorists in relation to this topic has been contradicted. So, Thomas Eager and Christopher Musso explain that the temperatures produced by the 9/11 attacks were certainly not high enough to make the steel structures that held up the buildings collapse but on the other hand that, as any expert on these materials knows well, steel loses 50% of its strength at 650°C and up to 90% at temperatures nearing 980°C [EAG 06]. Then we only need to add, as Phil Mole did, that the weakening of the general structure, caused by the collision and the fire, perfectly explains how the buildings collapsed [MOL 07].

To refute even one of these arguments demands a considerable commitment for anyone who is not an expert on these matters and, the larger the number of arguments, the harder for our mind to doubt in a general way the propositions made by these conspiracy theorists. This leads us back, once again, to the simple matter of motivation. We cannot reasonably expect the ordinary person to agree in order to devote as much time to these questions as the believer does. Once again we can find Olson's paradox, which allows a small group of motivated people to take over a non-representational space in the cognitive market.

Olson's paradox is understandably amplified when the amount of commitment (in this case to make a belief lose ground, and to create and memorize a line of argument that can be used to refute conspiracy theories) grows exponentially. Now, this is precisely what Fortean products occasion. Not only do they strengthen the credibility of conspiracy theories, but they also produce, on account of their sheer breadth, a sort of intimidation in all of those who would like to weaken them. When faced with this intimidation, how can the ordinary man or woman react? There are three kinds of possible answers.

First, he or she can refuse to believe and give up on the argumentative battle altogether. Faced with the believers' claims, he/she may shrug his/her shoulders and use irony, but he/she will often be aware of the illegitimate nature of his\her reaction. In fact it is quite hard to reject an idea on the pretext of its unreasonableness when we have nothing reasonable ourselves to set against a torrent of arguments. This situation may at least seem slightly awkward to him/her and he/she may try to put an end to this discomfort by saying: "Well, I'm not interested in your stories, tell someone else about them." However, this unease may as well be the first step toward a more ambiguous form of mental availability.

Second, he/she may claim to suspend judgment because of his/her inability to argue against the belief. To remain consistent, he/she may claim to have no point of view on the matter and postpone until later the moment when he/she has to form an opinion. He/she may then actually look for information and risk, if he/she searches the Net, being faced with the believers' cognitive oligopoly, thus either sliding into the third category or, quite the opposite, finding information that will help him/her go back to the first option. But he/she may as well, which is the likeliest outcome, given the amount of commitment entailed, avoid searching for information altogether and gradually cultivate the idea that there must be a grain of truth in these conspiracy theories and in this outlook, which is systematically suspicious of any official utterance. Without having turned into a believer, he/she may still reply to skeptical people that "things are complicated", a conclusion which is less the expression of his\her wisdom than that of his/her cognitive avarice.

Third, he/she runs the risk of becoming a believer him or her elf, having no desire or means to develop arguments against the believers' propositions.

2.18. Would you believe it!

The Internet enables, as we saw, the open sedimentation and the equally free circulation of layered lines of argumentation not authorized by the spoken word, which tends to "strip" accounts of everything but their structural stereotypes. Fortean products are the result of an incubation period that makes them alarming, but their argumentative structure gives rise to another equally frightening mental effect. It is produced by the concurrence of all these arguments and leads its endorses to say: "It cannot be a mere coincidence". Once we have a look at the videos, documents, and arguments of conspiracy theories, we can see how the concurrence of these arguments is often represented ironically. "Would you believe it!" is used to underscore the coincidence of several facts, all portrayed as disconcerting. This is the usual feeling produced by a large number of arguments converging on any given mind. As Lino Ventura said in *The Great Spy Chase* – Audiard was the screenwriter – "A beard is a beard, three beards make a spook!". Our impression that several coincidental events cannot be the result of mere chance reveals another problematic aspect of our brain's workings: our inability to properly evaluate unpredictable phenomena.

The technical means offered by the Internet for the sharing of arguments of belief stimulate this inability since, regardless of the quality of the evidence provided, they create *an impression of interdependence between these pieces of evidence* in such a way that, for those whose mind is willing to believe, the probability that they may lead to nothing approaches zero. The way we reason when faced with these kinds of cognitive products is approximately this: "It seems very unlikely that a set of n suspect elements may be used to back up this theory, unless there is something fishy going on.

We may admit that one of these elements is a simple coincidence, maybe two, but the whole lot of them?". Quite simply all of that seems so unlikely that we would be lying to ourselves if regarded it as a product of chance.

However, chance *and* the unpredictable are perfectly compatible; it is only a matter of *sample size*.

The miscalculation of sample size

Let us suppose that someone flipping a coin claims to have guessed right about the result 10 times in a row. This may seem strange insofar as it is unlikely, given that the odds of obtaining such a result are 977/1,000,000, i.e. slightly less than one out of 1,000. If this person showed this result to a panel on TV, he could give thousands of people the impression that this did not happen by mere chance and that mind powers do exist (in this case precognition). The only reasonable question we may ask this person is how many times he has flipped the coin in order to obtain this result. The (supposedly honest) answer we receive is 1,000 times! Subsequently there is no mystery anymore and the result obtained seems quite normal. This occurrence is indeed unlikely but it is the result of trial, which makes it nothing more than what we would normally expect from chance. By flaunting only the positive outcome and keeping secret the larger number of negative results, this person has flattered a banal mistake, made by our mind, which we may call *the miscalculation of sample size*. Thus it should come as no surprise for us that sometimes astrologists or clairvoyants make a right prediction, given both the number of predictions they make and the fact that they only publicize those that, by chance, hit the mark. More generally, the *miscalculation of sample size* takes place when we consider an event unlikely in itself but resulting from an immense number of occurrences. Then we regard it as extraordinary since we cannot, or are unwilling to, take into account the nature of the series out of which it resulted and we somehow isolate it from its context. Some coincidences seem so exceptional to us that we find it reasonable not to consider them a product of chance. The problem is that a phenomenon may be extraordinary (i.e. unlikely to happen) *and still* be a product of chance, provided that it is the result of a large number of occurrences.

The miscalculation of sample size is a widespread mental form of temptation and indeed not the only one that threatens our mind whenever it tries to grasp reality. New information technologies allow us to gain access (often visually) to phenomena. This kind of access is incomparably "wider" than it was in the past and automatically produces an enormous mass of data: the motivated believer will always be able to extract from this mass one or several facts that may be regarded as suspect, all the more easily since they will be isolated from the larger number of those that are not.

We only have to think about the countless pictures taken at the time of the 2001 attacks in New York against the Twin Towers. The collapse of the two buildings was filmed and photographed, and this tragic event created a substantial mass of data that anyone interested in finding out the truth behind the official version could compete to dissect. The actual truth sometimes being potluck, people end up finding what they actually seek. Watching the towers collapse, snapshot by snapshot, one was bound to see hidden shapes created by the curls of smoke caused by the fire. Why not the shape of the devil? Well, this is exactly what happened.

The *Philadelphia Daily News* featured an article on September 14th, 2001 that wondered whether Satan had actually "raised his hideous head" in the ashes of the attacks occurred 3 days before. What justified such a preposterous question was an image, out of the countless photographs taken of those terrible events, in which it was possible to make out a sort of face in the smoke caused by the fire of the World Trade Center (Figure 2.1). The newspaper remarked how these curls of smoke seemed to "reveal Satan's face, his beard, his horns and his evil expression, which represented for many the awful nature of an act that wreaked havoc on a city that did not expect it".

Figure 2.1. *The devil shape and the 9/11 attacks*

Out of the thousands of pictures that might have been taken of this event, it should come as no surprise that one of them contains shapes resembling familiar things. It is what we often did with clouds when we were children. This ability to see shapes where there are none is called *pareidolia* and is nothing more than a mental reflex. However, when a motivated mind is faced with these thousands of photographs, its chances of giving in to this reflex inevitably increase. What these pictures show, together with any kind of data, is our tendency to organize the information that makes up our reality. As believers will focus their attention on elements they can "exploit" as far as their belief goes, while disregarding the larger number of unusable facts, they start thinking that it cannot simply be a matter of coincidence. It is exactly this mental process that led a journalist, who undoubtedly started off with good intentions, to believe that the Bible contained secret prophetic messages.

2.19. It is all in the Bible, all of it

Gematria is a doctrine claiming to give an interpretation of sacred texts based on a numerical transcription of the value of each letter in order to discover their hidden meaning. Those who decide to devote themselves to this cryptological obsession will soon be struck, whatever their reading techniques, by extraordinary coincidences. By doing that they will also strike the imagination of a very large readership, since Gematria has inspired some nice best-sellers and can still guarantee a substantial profit for any unscrupulous publisher. One of the numerous examples is Robert Gold's *God and Π*, which claims to prove that "the decimals of Π represent the world's genome" by unearthing, even obsessively, traces of Π throughout the Ancient Testament. *The Bible Code*[22], a world bestseller written by American journalist Michael Drosnin, is even more appalling. According to him, the holy text of Judaism and Christianity is coded and hides some incredible prophecies that anticipate Hitler's rise to power as well as President Kennedy's murder, or even Itzak Rabin's assassination in 1995 at the hands of Ygal Amir. Should someone know the "secret code of the Bible", he or she would be aware that the extinction of the dinosaurs also figures in the narration. These cryptological approaches to sacred texts are nothing new. Somehow, these attempts started with Kabbala, which claims to attribute a number or a symbol to every letter of the Hebrew alphabet or, in other terms, to unearth a *code* that enables the reader to find out the real meaning behind

---

22 On this point see Patrick Berger's excellent file, from which I draw inspiration on this matter, on this website: http://www.zetetique.ldh.org/code_bible.html.

the surface. This tradition has continued uninterruptedly ever since the 13th Century and, in the first part of the 20th Century, rabbi Michael Ben Weissmandel carried out similar research on the Ancient Testament. However, we will focus here on one of his disciples, Eliyahu Rips, who carried on his teacher's work by making use of IT from the 1980s onwards [WIT 94]. The power introduced by computation is much superior to the combined analytical abilities of the Gematria researchers. From then on, the discovery of coded messages encrypted in the Bible speeds up. The technique employed is actually quite simple, yet so time consuming that only a computer can carry out the task in a short time. For example researchers decide, for a text, to only keep track of one letter every 12, nine, five, etc. or, in other terms, of "equidistant" letters. The chosen interval between each letter is of no consequence since researches working on Gematria will mainly keep track of those combinations that allow them to extract the most spectacular messages. So we can decide, as a rule for the word "superstition", to take into account only one in every two letters, which will give us the meaningless word "SUPERSTITION", i.e. **SPRTTO**. In some cases, however, words formed like this may have a meaning, or even make up coherent sentences. What should we think? Journalist Michael Drosnin was hesitant at first. He claims he was convinced by Eliyahu Rips when the latter managed to show him how the Torah had predicted the Iraq wars. The journalist, from skeptical, turns into a disciple of Gematria, so much so that in 2003 he publishes a second volume, *The Bible Code II*, which is equally well-received. He says that he was persuaded to write this book when, after the 9/11 attacks, he started using his computer to search the Bible for evidence of major events. He was soon able to read on his screen, stupefied, the words "twin", "towers", "plane", "it caused the collapse" and "twice". By now there was no doubt on his mind that someone had, in the very distant past, inserted prophetic messages into the Bible. What is the matter about? Drosnin tends to consider it more the sign of an alien civilization than God's, which is something, in either case, that does not have to do with my point. The main argument supported by Michael Drosnin, Eliyahu Rips and their colleagues is that the chances of such messages appearing in the Bible are so slim that the results obtained cannot be the product of mere coincidence. These claims can persuade the general public, who lack the means to counter them and who easily fall prey to the miscalculation of sample size, but leave a number of people, among whom mathematicians and statisticians, skeptical. Then Drosning inadvertently provides them with an idea that will be fatal to his theory, as he does in *Newsweek* while assuring readers that it is impossible to discover such coded messages in any other book but the Bible. He claims: "When my critics find a message about the assassination of a prime minister encrypted in *Moby Dick*, I'll believe them". That was all it took for Brendan McKay, mathematics professor at the National University of Australia, to buckle down [MCK 99].

While abiding by the cryptological rules set by *The Bible Code*, he starts carrying out research on *Moby Dick*. His discoveries undermine the journalist's prophetical ambitions. No fewer than nine messages about the assassination of a prime minister, among which Itzak Rabin's, are coded in this famous novel. McKay also discovers, encrypted in the novel, Lady Diana's death together with the name of her lover and that of their chauffeur. The claims advanced by Michael Drosnin and Eliyahu Rips constituted an intellectual bluff. Contrary to what they said, it was indeed possible to find any sort of random message in *Moby Dick*, provided one devoted enough time to it and owned a powerful computer. Besides, it is Drosnin himself who provides the most blatant contradiction to his own theory by predicting, in the second volume of his Gematria-related exercises, a nuclear war in the Middle East... for 2006.

Thus, it is possible to find words, even coherent sentences, in whatever kind of book by applying an arbitrary system of decryption. However, this discussion does not emphasize how, most of the time, we find a considerably larger number of incoherent phrases and meaningless letter clusters. Whenever a computer is used, the worthless and enormous amount of waste produced by this method of decryption is concealed. McKay's experiment would be enough in itself to end the discussion, but other mathematicians also made an effort to show the fragility of the theses put forward by Michael Drosnin and Eliyahu Rips. By applying to the Bible the above-mentioned reading technique that only takes into account equidistant letters, Doctor James Price was able to find such messages as: "God is odious", "hate Jesus", and even such contradictions as: "There is a God" and "There is no God".

This example seems particularly enlightening to me since it reproduces, on a much smaller scale, the way technical progress can serve the believer's will to considerably widen the spectrum of facts he or she as evidence. The miscalculation of sample size is an immutable feature of our way of thinking and yet we could free ourselves, with some organization, from its influence on us, were it not for the fact that the conditions of our information-based modernity strengthen, rather than inhibit, this mental state of confusion.

2.20. The transparency paradox

The power of technology nowadays does not only enable us to scan the Bible for "evidence" but also, somehow, to scrutinize the whole world. So Mohamed Al-Faiz, the manager of the Islamic Studies Center in Colombo (Sri Lanka), claimed he had seen Allah's name written in Arabic on the receding surf and foam of the deadly wave that hit Asia at the end of 2004. At least according to what he said to *Al-Arab*, a London newspaper. Those who made a point of verifying Mr Al-Faiz's claims never even started to believe that the fatal wave had shaped anything at all. Ahmed Halli, quite ironically, declared on *Le Soir d'Algerie* (January 2005) that, as a good Muslim, he actually examined these pictures and saw nothing miraculous in them. We have to admit to this journalist that it does take some imagination to see a parallel between this wave and Allah's name written in Arabic. Imagination and the will to believe that a tragedy that created hundreds of thousands of victims cannot be meaningless. The manager of the Islamic Studies Center in Colombo is blunt in his claim that the tidal wave is a punishment: "God has written his name and chastised those who ignored his laws". Be that as it may, it was satellite pictures, taken when the tidal wave hit the West coast of Sri Lanka which made this exercise in pareidolia possible. In this case, out of the countless photographs of the accident, Al-Faiz only chose those that could vaguely stimulate his religious belief. This is exactly how billions of visual aids worldwide now support the empire of beliefs. So, Google Moon (a service that shows satellite images of the Moon) provided some patient people with a shot in which they seriously believed they could see a man leisurely strolling on the lunar surface. While actually nothing more than the shade cast by a hillock, this mysterious apparition was shared all over the Net, in whose wake followed, as is often the case now, the wildest imaginings. The same goes for all those things that people imagine to have seen on Mars ever since the small rover *Curiosity* roamed all over it and sent us several shots of the red planet (mysterious light, totem, humanoid, etc.). There are then billions of eyes simultaneously scrutinizing our planet as well as the sky, ready to justify any interpretation.

Yes billions… the estimate is not off the mark. Thus nearly every modern cell phone can take pictures or videos, countless documents that will afterwards circulate all over the Internet. In 1997, there were no more than 210 million cell phone users, whereas now there are more than 5 billion, each of whom has the potential to record a segment of reality. These devices have mostly taken over the first video cameras, which appeared on the market at the end of 1970s, were popularized during the

1980s, and are still numerous, besides the fact that most cameras can also record. There are 10 million CCTV cameras worldwide, of which there are currently more than 300,000 in France, although the number is supposed to reach a million soon. The possibility to record a part of reality and spread it around a global network, with no significant costs involved and in record time, exponentially enlarges the sample size of reality from which believers can draw, each more than the next. The number of pictures posted every year on Flickr is estimated at 1 billion[23] whereas for Facebook the figure goes up to 2.5 billion. The average American internet user watches 182 videos a month. *The Economist* recalled, in its 02/27/10 feature, how contemporary societies were experiencing a "data flood" and how this accumulation and dissemination of mass-information had a great impact on our daily lives. If we stop and think about it, humankind produced 150 exabits of data in 2005, which is already an enormous figure, but in 2010 the number had increased eight times...

The believer is naturally motivated but, on his/her own, he/she would collapse like anyone else under this heap of information. However, it only takes one of them to find a single nugget of information in the mass of dross to occasion immediate data sharing. Since many others do the same worldwide, after a few weeks or months, although usually less, highly competitive Fortean products start appearing on the cognitive market. It is this way that, by tirelessly scrutinizing the countless images of Michael Jackson's death, people ended up noticing a movement of the sheet that covered his motionless body being carried to the hospital on a stretcher. This will be added to other arguments surfacing due to the commitment of the self-styled believers and will soon create an argumentative monster, as we saw above.

It goes without saying that these technological aids, which allow us to go beyond the limits of common sensory perception, are not exclusively used for the dissemination of beliefs. They establish technically what some have called, sometimes with joy and sometimes in fear, the *society of transparency.*

Sometimes they provide us with anecdotic information, which nonetheless will be shared all over the world, as happened in February 2010, when Sarah Palin was caught red-handed with a cheat sheet scrawled on the palm of her left hand at a Tea Party Convention. The Alaska governor had

---

23 http://blog.slate.fr/labo-journalisme-sciences-po/2010/02/13/le-pouvoir-de-reconnection-des-images-numeriques

put herself in an awkward situation because of the trivial nature of the words that were supposed to help her out: "energy", "tax", "American spirit" and "budget cuts". The situation was all the more embarrassing since Palin had just finished mocking Obama for relying too much, according to her, on autocue.

Some other times it is pictures taken on a cell phone and showing the abuse suffered by some prisoners in the Abou Ghraib jail, during the second Iraq war, that will move public opinion all over the world. We could come up with many more examples of how the society of transparency organizes every sort of opposition to official power. The most significant one is undoubtedly the mesh of lies in which Spanish prime minister José Maria Aznar got caught in after the Madrid attacks on March 11th 2004. While the election campaign was in full swing and polls announced the victory of the Popular Party at the general elections, several bombs exploded on a train at Atocha station, resulting in 190 casualties. There were two possible culprits, ETA or Al-Qaida. The Spanish army's involvement in the second Iraq war had not been especially appreciated by the country's public opinion (80% of Spaniards declared to be against it). Consequently, if these attacks had been carried out by Islamists keen on punishing Spain, this would have certainly not helped the situation for the government. Thus Aznar, with the general consensus of the traditional media, would support the ETA hypothesis stubbornly (he personally called the different newsrooms of the most important Spanish newspapers to make sure that it was this version that would be supported). What happened next made it clear that it was a lie, but the government only needed to hold out for a few days until the election day, which was scheduled on March 14th. However, the consensus of the traditional media was not enough for this deception to last long enough. The Internet traffic had multiplied eightfold since the day of the attack [THO 04]! Chats and forums were buzzing while websites dedicated to alternative sources of information were taken by storm (www.vilaweb.com, www.iblnews.com, www.indymedia.org). In addition to this, Internet users turned to the websites of international newspapers, which gave a very different interpretation in relation to the theories proposed for this attacks (on the CNN, MP Jack Straw declared he was sure about the Islamist hypothesis).

On March 14th, the election results are incontrovertible: the Popular Party 35 seats and the majority, whereas up to a few days before this affair it was winning the polls.

The Spanish Popular Party's unlucky attempt has become highly significant since it shows how hard it is for a politician, contrary to popular opinion, to keep a lie of that kind hidden for long. The government needed to hold out only for a few days, which was too long. This is why most conspiracy myths are not credible if we distance ourselves from the mass of arguments they support. The notion that a plot as elaborate as the one that might have led to the 9/11 attacks, involving as many accomplices, or entailing a coalition between governments and alien civilizations, or even enabling the United States to strike Japan in 2011 with a terrible earthquake due to a secret weapon could be kept secret is extremely unlikely. How can we explain, for example, the fact that no conclusive documents on this or that plot have been published on Wikileaks, which guarantees the anonymity of its contributors? Unless we suppose, of course, that even this website is in on the plot... which will be certainly deemed plausible by those readers who are reading these lines and are sensitive to conspiracy theories.

This leads us to a possible definition of the transparency paradox: any piece of information is now likelier than ever to enter the public domain, even when it constitutes an attempt to manipulate opinions. This exposure, given to even the most trivial of these attempts, gives the impression that their number is increasingly growing, whereas this transparency is actually a form of intimidation with the potential to reduce it! Anyone falling prey to this transparency paradox is victim of the *proportionality bias*.

The proportionality bias

This bias promotes the false idea that if we notice an amplification of the expression of a certain phenomenon we automatically think that the number of occurrences of this phenomenon has increased, unaware that this increase may be merely the result of improved observational tools. Thus, many are persuaded that the number of cancers diagnosed is much larger than it was in the past (which they regard as evidence of the contamination of our environment and food), unaware that part of this perceived increase results from the better performance of medical imaging and from the introduction of prevention campaigns (since in this case it is mainly a question of breast or prostate cancer). They are also unaware that this increase also depends on population ageing.

The proportionality bias lies then at the heart of the transparency paradox and gives our mind the impression that we are being lied to. We have no reason to think that there are more attempts to manipulate opinions than before, it is simply a matter of the fact that these attempts are more noticeable and advertised.

2.21. A shorter incubation period

On January 12th, 2010 a terrible 7.3-magnitude earthquake shook Haiti and resulted in more than 200,000 casualties. This is one of the poorest countries in the world and the tragedy might have plausibly seemed a horrible stroke of bad luck. Seismic events are hard to predict and control, but this is not everyone's opinion. So, only 10 days after the tragic event, an article supporting the notion that this earthquake had little to do with chance appeared on the website of Voltaire network. Once again, brandishing the "right to doubt" as a weapon of intimidation, Thierry Meyssan, who had also created the 9/11 conspiracy myth on the same website, wondered whether it was actually the United States which had provoked this earthquake[24]. According to him, the United States could technically do something of that sort. From the 1970s onwards, this country has carried out research on seismic weapons and its army now deploys "plasma and resonance impulse generators, combined with blast wave bombs" (sic). He also wonders, have we not seen strange American naval activities carried out in the Caribbean ever since 2008? Since Haiti's location was geopolitically important for the USA, this earthquake would have allowed the powerful country to invade the island on the pretext of false humanitarian reasons. Behind this conspiracy hypothesis, we can find a widespread fantasy about research called High Frequency Active Auroral Research Program (HAARP). This acronym refers to a kind of scientific and military research carried out by the USA whose aim was to understand the mechanisms regulating the ionosphere (an outer region of the atmosphere). The goal of this program, run by the University of Alaska, was mainly to improve long-range communication. It may be the case that the planners of this research have other intentions, but the notion that such an instrument might generate earthquakes would be risible, were it not that it also has to do with such tragic events as these deadly earthquakes. By now no seismic event, tsunami, or weather anomaly can happen without the HAARP's shadow hovering over the conspiracy imagination. Conspiracy theorists take this idea very seriously and mention some mysterious reports from Russia's Northern Fleet that could establish the facts and show the correlation between activities detected in the ionosphere and the seismic events that took place in Haiti at the beginning of 2010.

They actually draw their inspiration from a book coauthored by Jeane Manning and Nick Begich, called *Angels Don't Play This HAARP* and

---

24 http://www.voltairenet.org/Haiti-et-l-arme-sismique.

published in 1995, which supports the theory that this program is much more dangerous than the official version would have us believe. According to the authors, this project does not only aim to control the sky and the seismic dimension, but also human minds! Due to wave control, the USA is ready to subjugate our brains whenever it thinks fit. I would not have mentioned this book or this theory, were it not that the term "Haarp" has become a simple linguistic indicator that can show the appearance of a conspiracy theory after a seismic event. This traceability of the conspiracy hypothesis, due to the term "Haarp", allows us to focus on one of the many ways the revolution of the information market favors collective credulity. Formerly, a certain "incubation" period was needed for the development of a conspiracy theory. If an upsetting event happened – such as a mysterious assassination, a disappearance, or a natural catastrophe – a conspiracy theory might have developed, usually slowly by word of mouth. As the news world is now fast and a topic brushes aside the next, most events, unless they were especially traumatizing, barely excite the conspiracy theorists' imagination. This imagination somehow lacked the time necessary for the sedimentation of a good story, which needed too much time for its dissemination, so the interest it had provoked could not last. The dissemination speed of conspiracy hypothesis is fundamental for its chances of propagating and lasting. Evidently, the Internet contributes majorly to the ability of conspiracy myths to spread breathtakingly quickly.

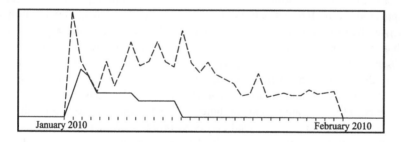

Figure 2.2. *Searches on Google for the words "Haiti earthquake" (dotted) and "HAARP"*

If we recall the earthquake that hit Haiti on January 12th, 2010 and examine Internet users' searches on Google during January and February 2010, the following graph will show us two things. On the one hand, the dotted line representing searches carried out for the words "earthquake/Haiti", indicates how from January 13th onwards users have extensively been looking for information about the event. On the other hand, the other curve shows how, starting on Thursday 14th January, users have begun to search all over the Net for links between the earthquake and HAARP!

The graph also shows us how users (at least French-speaking users) were only worried about the event until the end of January, whereas HAARP-related concerns were present until the end of February. Undoubtedly, this demand for conspiracy links could not be met at first but it was soon afterwards satisfied by the supply we have talked about (to which Meyssan contributed, among others).

The time it takes it to disseminate information is then essential to the strength of the empire of beliefs. By now, the hypothesis of a correlation between this earthquake and HAARP is available on the Net and will remain available for everyone, even if the event will soon seem old. According to a "Fortian" process, which we now know well, this event will add to a line of argument that is built like a *mille-feuilles*: despite the shakiness of every layer – taken singularly – the overall impression that a general observer receives is one of solidity.

Now conspiracy myths can appear a few days, or even hours, after the occurrence of the events they draw from. For instance, a conspiracy theory in relation to the May Sofitel affair, which involved Dominique Strauss-Kahn, appeared on the Internet only hours after facts had been made public. In this sense, the most striking example is undoubtedly the torrent of crazy theories that appeared merely hours after the deadly attack on French satire magazine *Charlie Hebdo*, which would later catch the world's attention. On January 7th, 2015, the day when the attacks took place, there were already 26 arguments pertaining to conspiracy theories! The day afterwards, on Janaury 8th, 21 additional arguments were available to establish an alternative version of the official events according to which these attacks had been perpetrated by two young radical Islamist brothers. Some claimed that the color of the wing mirrors of the murderers' car had changed, while others thought that the President of the Republic had arrived too quickly on the scene (he must have known already), etc. Through their collaboration, their meticulous study of all the anomalies that could be found in the available pictures and videos of the accident, and of course their will to believe, they helped give a spine-chilling example of a Fortian product in the making. The following graph shows the increase in the number of conspiracy-related arguments available on the cognitive market day by day.

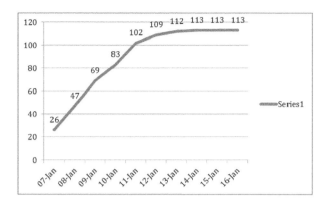

Figure 2.3. *Conspiracy-related arguments after the Charlie Hebdo attacks*

Thousands of such stories can be found on the Internet but, if they are in any way relevant to the purpose of this book, it is more because they stress the new conditions for the formation of beliefs than they amuse the reader.

First of all, they can illustrate how an increased dissemination of information allows certain fabrications to last longer, whereas in other circumstances they could have never appeared on the cognitive market or, in any case, would have been short-lived.

Afterwards, they show how the spectrum of subjects that can give rise to beliefs, rumors and conspiracy theories has widened, which automatically increases the belief rate across the social space.

Last, they enhance the ramifying nature of the conspiracy theory, which feeds on everything and tends to appear on the cognitive market in the shape of Fortian products.

This reduction in the incubation period necessary for the appearance of unverified accounts on any topic puts such pressure, due to the Internet, on the competition that the traditional media cannot always keep up with. This situation is a cog in the wheel that favors the advent of the believers' democracy and underlines how competition in the field of information does not always promote truth-telling, as we are going to see.

Competition Serves the Truth,
Excessive Competition Harms It

3.1. Michael Jackson's son, abused by Nicolas Sarkozy

It is May 22nd 2003 and on the 8 o'clock news on *TF1* a young man, Djamel, is making serious accusations against Dominique Baudis. He claims he has witnessed sex parties, held by prominent citizens of Toulouse, in which children were sexually abused and even murdered. The "Toulouse affair" is in full swing and the whole of France is buzzing with the rumor that the ex-mayor of that town has protected a serial killer, Patrice Allègre, and has engaged with him and other city notables in orgies involving prostitutes and children.

That night, the news desk of *TF1* (the *France 2* news desk would follow suit on the 24th) decided to give Djamel the floor during peak viewing time. For those who did not see this in real time, it is evident that these accounts resemble all those urban myths that accuse the middle class of the worst abuses. However, at the time commentators did not find this blatant at all. Rather than showing some circumspection, as such circumstances should require, and verifying the most trivial piece of information before making it public, the French media, with few exceptions, gave in to this affair without any deontological consideration.

Is there any need to recall that Djamel also claimed, off the record, that he was Michael Jackson's secret son and that he had been sexually abused by several French ministers, not least Nicolas Sarkozy, and show business personalities? How could we give such a character the floor during peak viewing time? And what blindness led people to cut from the interview the most implausible moments, which would have stripped this young man of his credibility and openly shown that he was a compulsive liar[1]?

The Baudis/Allègre affair is the French textbook case of media deterioration. Quite a complex affair, it starts at the beginning of the 2000s with the zeal of a policeman called Roussel, who was convinced that not all of the crimes committed by Patrice Allègre, a French serial killer, had been discovered, especially because of the 7 year gap in his criminal biography. This blank period led chief warrant officer Roussel to believe that there might be unsolved murders or disappearances, maybe at the hand of a serial killer. With the help of a computer program, he tried to link a whole series of mysterious crimes to the serial killer's record and, due to the testimony of several prostitutes, he thought he was about to discover a horrifying plot, which would soon afterward delight the French media. I will not explain this affair, which lasted several years, in detail here[2], but we can recall that numerous pieces of pseudo evidence and cognitive prejudices have led to the creation of this myth. It would also be easy to identify in this affair the consequences of the *Fortian effect*, since even after all the ex-prostitutes' accusations had been invalidated, some kept stating that: "there must be a grain of truth in it". This is exactly what happened to policeman Roussel in January 2004. Once again, it is fascinating to see how, despite every element of the case being poorly backed up, the general impression still favored the conspiracy hypothesis on the sole basis that the main accusation was supported by a large number of wild imaginings passed off as facts. In Tolouse, there was even an association which attempted to uncover this plot, evocatively called: *There's no smoke without fire*.

What is striking, apart from this Fortean effect, is the behavior of the media. For this reason, this example makes the perfect introduction to this chapter. In France, very few managed not be affected by the conspiracy-related hypotheses or by the actual accusations. The main reason is that none of us was wise enough to seriously verify the information they provided. Once an affair has become this important and once it provokes such a demand from public opinion, journalists may be tempted, being in a

---

1 This was, for example, the stance taken by Robert Namias, news director for *TF1* at the time, who explains that they made a point of bowdlerizing Djamel's account a little. See [ETC 05, p. 263].
2 This affair is meticulously described in [ETC 05].

condition of extremely fierce competition, to publish according to their feelings and inmost convictions. They start betting on the truth. Subsequently, journalists become like everyone else: confined to the boundaries of their rationality and vulnerable to the appeal of adulterated products on the cognitive market. It must also be added that it is in their interest to publish saucy or scandalous affairs, which is demonstrated by the testimony of Florence Bouquillat, who had recorded Djamel's declarations for *France 2* and who had been asked by his superiors, upset about being beaten to it by *TF1*, to broadcast those images[3]. The journalist, when asked about Djamel's credibility, claims that she had noticed the prostitute's unreliability but that this did not imply that everything he said was untruthful. Besides, she also maintains that her superiors believed it was not her job to settle the question of how truthful or false a testimony might be.

Competition among information sources, which is a fundamental condition of democratic life, sometimes reveals its drawbacks when it becomes too fierce: it automatically entails a decreased amount of time dedicated to the verification of information[4]. This drop, in turn, increases the possibility that journalists may walk into every sort of mind trap: stereotypes, urban myths, cognitive prejudices, etc. But, I want to insist here on the fact that, despite the condemnatory nature of the examples I recall to put forward my thesis, journalists are not incriminated as a professional category: they react as most of us would in a similar situation. The crux of the matter is represented by the new conditions of the information market. As it happens, the distributors of information are caught in a sociocognitive trap that theorists of the trade know well. This trap has been tested experimentally in many ways and the average global answer corresponds more or less to the temptation.

3.2. A "prisoner's dilemma" kind of situation

The liberalization of the main media and their competition are natural and positive tendencies of democratic societies. Positive indeed since how could a democrat wish for anything different? These are the consequences of the

---

3 See the program *Arrêt sur image*, available at: http://www.arretsurimages.net/contenu.php?id=179.
4 Marchetti [MAR 10] shows in particular how this competitive effect has affected scientific journalism, especially in relation to health problems faced by journalists in real life. We call this *the prisoner's dilemma*.

receding of political power before the media. We may think that these two still go hand-in-hand and debate this point over and over, but we may never seriously support the idea that this situation can be compared to what happens in a dictatorship. This media *competition* is inherently *democratic*, yet this does not prevent the creation of pernicious effects, especially the way this competition favors a rhythm of information dissemination not always compatible with that of knowledge.

The idea which I will support in this section is that this situation of competition, together with the temporality of the dissemination of information it promotes, or more precisely the reduction in the amount of time dedicated to the verification of information, provokes a sharing of errors which will pass off as common sense. In other terms, these conditions will allow the dark side of our rationality to dominate the public space in relation to certain topics.

The traditional media (newspapers, radio and television), already in competition with each other, have been highly subjected to the competition introduced by the Internet. Thus, according to an Orange/Terra Femina survey carried out in 2011, 62% of respondents claim they resort to digital media to find information "as fast as possible", whereas another survey conducted by Ericsson in the same year reveals that 35% of Americans who own a smartphone start searching for information even before getting out of bed. This may seem anecdotal but it reveals quite well how all of those professions involved in the dissemination of information are part of this cut-throat competition. The key to their career success has to do, among other things, with how quickly they can share a piece of information. This has always been a cause of possible deterioration for this profession (finding a scoop at any cost, being tempted by sensationalism, etc.), but the modern conditions of the cognitive market force it to show sometimes the worst of itself. The resulting situation closely resembles the prisoner's dilemma.

The prisoner's dilemma

The prisoner's dilemma is a canonical example in game theory. It consists of an imaginary situation that can be described as follows. Two people (X and Y), having committed a crime together, are imprisoned separately and with no possibility of speaking to each other. Each accomplice is interrogated separately and does not know whether the other will betray him or remain silent. We know that, if X betrays Y but Y remains silent, X will be set free and Y will serve 10 years in jail, and *vice versa*. If they both betray each other, they will both serve 5 years in jail. If they both remain silent, they will serve 6 months each (for lack of tangible proof).

We can see how the best decision would be to remain silent and only serve the 6 months. However, not knowing what the other will do, a person may be very tempted to betray him and hope he will remain silent, which would result in his release. In fact, X and Y will reason in the same terms, which is far from irrational, and get 5 years in jail. If they had known how to cooperate, they would have certainly made a more advantageous choice. This dilemma is the distinguishing feature of all those situations where there is an optimal choice to be made but the subjects, being in competition, cannot cooperate and, while acting in their personal interest, will end up with a form of collective irrationality.

What elements make competition on the information market correspond to the prisoner's dilemma? As it turns out, a journalist or an editorial staff member with the opportunity to disseminate an unverified piece of information cannot avoid wondering whether their rivals will publish it or not. Their reasoning may then be outlined as follows (this pertains to the printed press, even if the line of reasoning is evidently the same for the other media):

1) *Situation A*: if we do not publish this piece of information and others do, we will give our readers the impression that they are less informed than other readers and, what is worse, that we withhold information.

2) *Situation B*: if we publish this piece of information and others do not, we will give our readers the impression that they are better informed than other readers and that our rivals withhold information.

3) *Situation C*: if we all publish this piece of information, we can curb the risks posed by competition, but if this piece of information is false we collectively lose our credibility as a profession.

4) *Situation D*: we decide not to publish this piece of information and our rivals do the same. This piece of information is invisible, costs and benefits are non-existent.

Several observations should be made. On the one hand, the consequences of each situation depend on whether the piece of information is true or false. So, situation A may, in the end, be advantageous to the media which decide not to publish this piece of information, if it turns out to be false. However, what reduces the competitive situation of the media to the prisoner's dilemma is that this kind of situation does not occur too often, for two reasons. The first reason has to do with how excessive competition between the distributors of information makes the position of the determined solitary abstainer very risky. Besides, who can remember the rare individual that remained circumspect once the majority of the profession has been led astray? Conversely, if the information proves to be true, this cautiousness will be deemed highly reprehensible.

The second reason is that uncertain public information empirically proves to be true more often than not (there are significant exceptions, such as the Toulouse affair itself and the fake anti-Semitic aggression on the RER in July 2004). This motivates journalists to try to come up with a scoop rather than taking the risk of leaving it to the competition, especially given that they can employ hypotheticals as a sort of lightning rod.

On the other hand, situation D is becoming rarer and rarer. So, in France, a tacit agreement between all the media, which lasted until the 1990s, made it possible to escape from the "prisoner's dilemma" situation imposed by the pressure of competition, at least in relation to topics concerning politicians' private lives. Once again, the advent of the Internet increases this pressure by allowing everyone to offer information on the cognitive market. Consequently, even the most trivial rumor, if it is somehow successful on this heterodox information market, exerts pressure on the traditional media and will jeopardize this tacit agreement, leading the media back to the problematic "prisoner's dilemma" condition.

3.3. Presidential unfaithfulness and the burnt Koran

On February 24th 2010, a freelance journalist and BFM Radio presenter posts a tweet that says out loud what everyone is thinking in Parisian newsrooms: "Here it is. The Biolay-Carla rumor has landed on Twitter. We've got a nice bullshit bingo ahead of us[5]". A few days later, hundreds of tweets will mention an affair that the whole world will soon hear about. Carla Bruni, then the French first lady, has left Nicolas Sarkozy for singer Benjamin Biolay. As for the President, he is finding comfort in the arms of the karateka Chantal Jouanno, none other than the State Secretary for the Environment. The thrills and spills of this affair, involving partner-exchanges between four well-known figures of the political and artistic world, make it the perfect media product. Except for the fact that to mention

---

5 The elements shown here are drawn from http://www.arretsurimages.net/ content.php?id=2813.

this officially would constitute a breach of the tacit agreement between the traditional media, which establishes that politicians' private lives cannot be discussed. At the same time, the tweets that mention the affair are often posted by journalists, which will seem paradoxical if we recall that social networks are supposed to be semi-private, allowing information to be treated very differently from the way the traditional media deal with it. Besides, this affair is mentioned in an ironic and humorous way, and only very rarely in explicit tones. This buzz becomes obsessive and some people soon get their hands on it on Websites or blogs. Thus, on March 5th, 2010, Arnauld Champremier-Trigano writes on blogact.com: "It runs, it runs, the love disease… it smells, it smells, the current news… It smells like the end between the President and Carla Bruni, who is going after a new love. So, why did I publish such a shitty rumor on my blog??? First of all because, if it's true that I couldn't verify the information, I've made a point of confirming that this rumor was circulating in many newsrooms and it was indeed. So at least it must be taken for what it is: a talking point and a concern for journalists". It is a new tweet, posted by Johann Hufnagel, which will amplify this trend. This journalist is deemed trustworthy, having worked for *Libération*, 20minutes.fr, and having been chief editor for the information Website Slate.fr. However, his tweet is enigmatic to say the least – "Benjamin Biolay is the guy who…" – and this is all it takes for another Website, Suchablog.com, to consider this enough evidence to start mentioning the rumor quite explicitly on March 8th 2010. The webmaster even believes he knows why journalists are not officially mentioning this "important" affair: "Several newsrooms are clearly aware of a little change in the dynamics of the presidential couple but will not publish this information before the regional elections… By now Carla Bruni is in love with singer Benjamin Biolay, nominated twice on Saturday night for the music awards, and has already moved in with him…".

The credibility of this rumor reaches a turning point on March 9th 2010 when a blog hosted by the Website *Journal du Dimanche* explicitly mentions the affair. The paper format of the famous weekly magazine does not give any room to the rumor, but the damage is done. The mere association with the name of the magazine seems to give this gossip enough credit and a wide enough audience to turn it into an international affair over the following days. *The Sun*, the *Daily Mail*, *La Nacion*, the *Irish Independent*, *La Stampa* and tens of other newspapers will mention the crisis of the French presidential couple. They are thoughtless enough to disregard the possibly conjectural nature of the information and do not point out that if the *Journal du dimanche* was indeed involved with this affair, it was because of a blog it hosted rather than its official format. Either way, the pressure is now too strong for the tacit agreement, which regulates the treatment of private matters, to be applied. The prisoner's dilemma is the prevailing way of thinking: no one wants to run the risk of not publishing this saucy piece of information if the competitors do. This strange affair, which would later turn out to be completely untruthful, was then mentioned on the pages of nearly all the French newspapers, radio and television. Naturally, people talked about it in very ironic terms and, most of the time, by bringing up the analysis of society and trying to find out why French politics, which had until then guarded against it, was about to be "mediatized". As historian Robert Zarestsky, professor at the University of Houston, remarks, it is not merely a matter of national culture since, even in the United States, until recently: "No one cared if Roosevelt or Eisenhower cheated on their wives. John F. Kennedy's affaires never caused a scandal. There were rumors on President George H.W. Bush that were never verified (…) If the situation in the United States has become like this, after Bill Clinton, it is in large part thanks to the Internet (…) and cable channels like Fox News…"[6].

Returning to France, every newsroom knew that François Mitterrand, President of the Republic, had a secret daughter but they kept the secret for ethical reasons. It is the same country where now it is enough for a tabloid to publish a picture of the President (François Hollande) on a scooter, on his way to see his mistress (Julie Gayet, a well-known actress in France), for the press to seize upon it.

On January 14th, 2014 during François Hollande's press conference, the head of the Presidential Press Association asks the first question about his private life in the very first few minutes: "Is Valérie Trierweiler still the first lady of France?". He will apologize immediately afterward with an explicit tweet: "Albert Londres, forgive me!". Subsequently, more than 20% of the questions asked by journalists will revolve around the alleged relationship between the President and the actress. The fierce competition, together with the lack of dialogue it entails, prevented the development of the common good. It even led the traditional media to associate themselves with themes they had refused to deal with in the past. In my opinion, we need to look no further than this "prisoner's dilemma" for the reasons of the "mediatization"

---

6 "Laxisme contre puritanisme", *Libération*, 18/05/11.

of politics. It only takes one to get involved for the rest to get sucked in. Now, the advent of the Internet and the revolution of cognitive supply it entails allows everyone to set the process in motion and the official media to mention facts while pointing out that it is, *of course*, only rumors. The vicious circle is then complete. There is now an extreme permeability between the conventional information market and the heterodox market of the Internet. This is particularly noticeable on news Websites, including those belonging to newspapers of the traditional press. Whereas formerly the press was not very sensible to public demand, it has moved on, over the course of a few years, to a strong type of indexation of the readership's demand. So, sociologist Angèle Christin, whose doctoral thesis[7] at Princeton revolved around this topic, underlines how programs such as Chartbeat, Visual revenue and XiTi (used to gauge the audience on the Internet) have become a sort of second editor in chief for these formats. Audience figures can, in fact, alter the editorial treatment of a topic. Even the titles of articles or their positions are modified in order to attract the regular customer. Unsurprisingly, the sociologist shows that most of the time it is the trashiest or most sensational topics, besides those having to do with sex or violence, which appeal the most. But there is more to it than that: due to the *scrolling patterns* analysis, we know that readers often go no further than the first two paragraphs, which promotes the writing of shorter and shorter articles.

Like the two inmates facing their judge, journalists know well that it would be better, in terms of information quality, not to spew out rumors, even the sauciest, on the cognitive market. They can *see* the common good but they cannot make it compatible with their *personal interest*. This is not impossible to do since some journalists and some media, depending on the matter, manage remarkably well and can certainly keep their job. However, they seem on average to be increasingly ensnared by the prisoner's dilemma.

To give another example, journalists all over the world must have known that it was absurd to pay so much attention to an unknown minister coming from Gainesville, who had been a nobody up to then and who owned all of his global "fame" to his clearly stated intention to burn some Korans. In 2010, minister Terry Jones asks anyone willing to listen to him (at first, there

---

7 "Clicks or Pulitzers? Web Journalists and Their Work in the United States and France" (Princeton – EHESS: unpublished thesis).

was only a handful of them) to send him some Korans, so that he can perform a purifying act of book burning on the symbolic date of 9/11 from 6 pm to 9 pm, as he points out. He is an odd character who was at the head of a Christian community in Germany at the end of the 1980s. During the years he spent in Germany, he was guilty of many financial irregularities and appropriated the title of "doctor". He already seemed an extremist to those who met him during this period but the name of the Pentecostal community he founded in Florida, the Dove World Outreach Center, does not actually reveal his aggressive disposition. He opened a Facebook account to celebrate his future pyromaniac feat, which soon reached 11,000 fans. This character is incendiary and provocative, evidently a suitable subject for a short report, but did that mean that he had to be shown on a loop on the screens of American televisions? In fact, everyone is well aware of how illogical it is to mediatize such a character, who can usually only rely on the support of his 30 odd followers. This fact is quite inconsequential but once again, if people talk about it, then everyone may be tempted to do it, predicting the demand. General Petraeus, who was leader of the NATO troops and commander of the ISAF in Afghanistan when this incident took place, even officially voiced his concerns about Terry Jones's project. The French media were no exception to this process of contamination, sometimes dealing with the matter in terms of society analysis and some others in figurative terms but, whichever the case, always facilitating the dissemination of a piece of information that everyone knew to be potentially dangerous *as well as* completely uninteresting. From a journalistic perspective, this piece of information could only become interesting if it led to consequences resulting from the fact that it had been mediatized illegitimately. This is exactly what almost happened, since not only did this minister and his community receive several death threats but, in Afghanistan, some violent demonstrations broke out to protest against this book-burning project. If we have a look at the Internet searches for "Terry Jones" carried out on Google at the time, we can see, unsurprisingly, that the largest demand comes from Indonesia, a major Muslim country, rather than Europe or the United States.

To give minister Jones such prominence was not only absurd, but also frankly reprehensible in terms of moral responsibility. Everyone was clearly aware that the dissemination of such a microscopic piece of information was disadvantageous to the common good, but only few were willing to counter the "prisoner's dilemma" logic in this matter. Clearly, the pressure of competition, whether it comes from the Internet, from the proliferation of channels due to cable television or from any other format, adds to the pressure that has always been exerted on professional distributors of information.

What the Terry Jones affair reveals is the bonus on which every agitator can now rely. Thus, we have reason to fear exaggerations in this field: what kind of tweet could I post to make it circulate? What kind of idea can I support on my blog to make sure that it will be promoted? What status on my Facebook account could help me make people talk about me? Without blaming those who communicate with a systematic cynicism, we can suppose that, *ceteris paribus*, the fierce competition around which the contemporary cognitive market pivots does not always favor moderation.

Some do not hesitate to employ this dilemma, which characterizes the media, to promote results that claim to be scientific and yet want to cut loose from the temporality necessary to rational examination. So, on September 19th 2012, Gilles-Eric Séralini, who had been trying to show the dangers posed by GMOs for several years, really exploited the press to give his results a stunning amount of publicity. We will return to what the scientific community thinks of this research, whose conclusions were presented as "revolutionary", but let us first recall the facts. Séralini had secretly conducted a study on rats supposed to demonstrate the dangers posed by a GMO: the NK 603. Rather than waiting for his published article to occasion second opinions and to become, or not become, a point of reference for his peers' community, he preferred to entrust the scientific text only to those journalists who would agree to sign a non-disclosure agreement, which prevented them from having it assessed by experts (which is actually the norm). He employed the prisoner's dilemma against journalism. In fact, they could either give in to the coercion or run the risk of missing out on an allegedly significant piece of scientific information. It goes without saying that, given the circumstances, a good percentage of them gave in to the coercion, which sometimes came with a warning. In the press and on the radio, one declaration followed the other: a major weekly magazine wrote "GMOs are poison", whereas a public radio station broadcasted "There's no doubt about it now, GMOs are dangerous". It was not a time for hypotheticals. By then, the dilemma already seemed to dominate every kind of commentator, since several politicians had made sensational declarations on the same day in favor of a request for a ban on GMOs. These intemperate commentators should have waited a little longer since, as we will see, the scientific community immediately reacted all over the world to express its suspicions and point out the unacceptable gaps in the experimental procedure, something Gilles-Eric Séralini had already been reproached for.

The situations that I have just described engage people in processes that are disadvantageous to the common good. These people are well aware of it but the prisoner's dilemma leads them to illustrate Ovid's famous sentence (*Metamorphoses*, VII, 20) – "*Video meliora proboque, deterio sequor*" ("I see better things, and approve, but I follow worse"). When it is only a matter of publicizing real or imaginary facts that are simply not worth it, the consequences are not significant, but the situation is completely different when the urgency with which information is disseminated provokes collective fears.

3.4. The IRC curve (information reliability/competition)

Were the Mayans right? Was the end of the world really about to come? It is a question that commentators loved asking semi-ironically until December 2012. However, it took quite a strange turn when the media, social networks and blogs all over the world reported the worrying news that a "supervolcano", until then inactive, had been discovered in Germany. This volcano threatened to wake up and spew out billions of tons of magma, thus burying a part of Europe and simultaneously changing the world as we know it. This giant volcano, called Laacher See (its name derives from its crater lake), is located in the *land* of Rhineland-Palatinate and its surface measures 1,605 km². It is supposed to wake up every other 10,000 years and the alarmist press claimed that experts thought a new eruption was imminent. Exactly what experts? In any case, it is certainly not geologists, who noticed no particular seismic activity in Germany. However, those made up for fun by the Daily Mail, which came up with this hoax, were unanimous: we are in great danger. This is then another example of how an adulterated piece of news can be disseminated breathtakingly fast on the cognitive market, without any authority or form of control being able to curb it. But this time, the case is particularly funny since the whole matter was a simple joke.

I want to state again clearly that if journalists are indeed often involved in the aforementioned examples, it is not because they are less virtuous than others. My intentions would be oddly misread if all of what I have said should be compared with those practices of "media criticism" that nondescript prosecutors delight in. If the part played by journalists is so significant in this section, it is because they are more than any other profession faced with the ambiguity regulating the relationships between information reliability and competition.

In fact, any other kind of profession, if similarly coerced, would be subjected to the same type of deterioration. Journalists do not constitute, in contemporary societies, the only profession injured by the urgency with which information is delivered; scientists do not always escape this constraint either, as the ill-fated story of a society called *IntegraGen* illustrates.

The topic of autism and its origins has given rise to much debate. This disease has long been considered as a psychological or psychoanalytic condition. According to traditional psychoanalysis, the mother was to blame since a lack of affection on her part could have led to the development of autism in some children. Progress in biology has allowed us to weaken this theory significantly. Step-by-step, the notion that this condition is in large part genetic has won over most experts [JAM 03]. In this context, when French company *Integragen* declared on July 19th, 2005 that it had developed the first diagnostic test for autism, it was a complete shock. This test claimed to be based on the presence of four genes, including the PRKCB1, directly involved in the etiology of this condition. However, several years after this declaration was made, no new results have been published. The 2005 statements have disappeared from the company's Website and, in general, everything shows that they were largely premature, as Jourdan underlines [JOU 07]. Why such haste? The fact is that *IntraGen* is a biotechnology start-up. These companies are in most cases recently founded, small-sized and financed by "venture capitalists". Thus, they are expected to produce convincing results in the short run since, at the beginning, they lose considerable amounts of money. These companies effectively employ this latency period by carrying on research and come up with a molecule, a measuring device or a test, as is the case here, which will open up lucrative markets. Those who have invested in these companies desire a quick return on investment and the latter are pressurized into announcing results they have not yet obtained. They are then put in a situation characterized by the urgency with which information is disseminated, which, as is the case here, may lead to unfortunate consequences.

Similarly, was it really necessary to announce on September 23rd, 2011, as the 200 physicists involved in the "Opera" experiment did, that neutrinos were faster than the speed of light? The experiment consisted of measuring the time these particles took to travel the 730 km that separate the CERN from an Italian detector set up for this purpose. Over the course of these experiments, neutrinos arrived 60 billionths of a second sooner than it was theoretically predicted, since the "journey" was supposed to last 3 ms. It was not then a trivial announcement since, had it been confirmed, it would have shaken the whole system of Einsteinian theoretical physics. We may hope that the more significant the theoretical or practical consequences of a declaration, the more prudent the statement itself. In fact, this revolution expected in the field of physics, as people would learn a few months later, was not a revolution at all. These remarkable, yet false, results were the consequence of a GPS that was not properly connected. In the meantime, obviously, the news spread all over the world. In France, *Le Monde* published, for the occasion, an editorial by Hervé Morin [MOR 11], who thought that the CNRS and CERN researches were a nice example of ethicality: "Faced with results that upset the comfortable routine of certainties, the physicists involved in this experiment could have kept their works to themselves. They have instead chosen to do the opposite". Science is not spared by the consequences we can expect from the prisoner's dilemma, that regulate the relationships between information reliability and degree of competition. Besides, the article about the superluminal neutrinos was first published by a Website called ArXiv.org, which was certainly not on par with peer-review journals. Thus, only the inflexible norms regulating the relationships between those involved in the same social space can counter the tendency prevailing on the other cognitive markets, on their way to deregulation. So far, the scientific field has held out against it but, as this example shows, its defenses are getting weaker. When competition reaches a *certain degree*, the pressure exerted on the dissemination of information is such that the likeliness of information reliability tends to decrease. This does not mean that the amount of adulterated pieces of information is more substantial, but that these pieces of information are more easily disseminated.

I have specifically pointed out that this happens when a *certain degree of competition* is reached, as it is a common knowledge that the cognitive monopoly that any dictatorship in the world has ever tried to establish never favored the promotion of truth. A certain degree of competition on the cognitive market is actually necessary to information reliability but, as the general title of this section points out: *competition serves the truth, excessive competition harms it*. The following graph broadly outlines the relationship between information reliability and degree of competition.

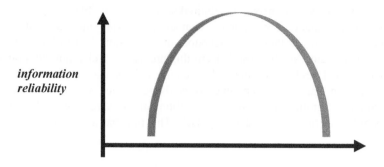

information
reliability

Figure 3.1. *Degree of competition*

As we can see, the degree of competition on the cognitive market, by assumption, augments the average reliability of information but, at a certain degree, it tends to occasion its drop for two main reasons, which I am going to recall as a conclusion to this section.

On the one hand, the pressure exerted by competition decreases the average time devoted to the verification of information, which is especially problematic when the matter in question possesses a technical dimension that should encourage us to dedicate time to its analysis (this is especially the case for those topics – environment or health-related subjects – on which now the orthodoxy of science has often lost its grip in the public space).

On the other hand – this is the most important point – the pressure exerted by competition, as we have seen in several examples, encourages people to give in more easily to the least honorable inclinations of the human mind, a phenomenon we might call cognitive demagogy. Thus, these are the perfect conditions for a sort of generalized sharing of mistakes about crucial matters. I do not think that this sharing happened accidentally in our history. It was not coincidental that we welcomed the premature claim that neutrinos were faster than the speed of light. We gave our approval while demanding that other professions follow the lead of these virtuous scientists, who were not afraid to revolutionize with such claims the intellectual program that had, up to then, enabled us to understand the world. Hervé Morin, in his editorial published on *Le Monde*, argues that: "Healthcare scandals, incompetent experts, corruption and conflicts of interests have been tarnishing the scientists' reputation with the general public for several years. What is currently happening in the physicists' community is, on the contrary, a remarkable display of the integrity of the scientific method".

Many of these commentators admired how it was possible to express such mistrust and found it profoundly democratic. Taking into account what happened afterward, these commentators may be astonished to know that I agree with them. Not because I deem this premature declaration admirable, but because I find it extremely democratic. I think that the best political system man has ever been able to envisage carried with it something potentially harmful – the technical conditions of its expression – which was only biding its time before revealing itself. That time has now come.

4

What Can Be Done? From the Democracy of the Gullible to the Democracy of Enlightenment

4.1. The hope of the astrophysicist

On September 25th 2011, at *France Inter*, I was invited to discuss, with a renowned astrophysicist, the relationship between science and belief. My interlocutor was André Brahic, a researcher who discovered the Neptune rings, and was a member of the scientific teams in the *Cassini* and *Voyager* missions. A specialist of our solar system, he has, among other things, written splendid works about the planets that we are familiar with. We went over some of the strange beliefs that pervade our contemporary world and we had to inevitably ask ourselves the question: why? Why have beliefs not been weeded out from a world where science exists and knowledge never stops making progress? André Brahic had ideas about a lot of topics and he has one about this matter. In his opinion, there was an irrational part in the human spirit and that could undoubtedly be undermined due to education. People embrace questionable ideas because they do not have enough education. We did not debate too much this rather technical point, but undoubtedly this was the only disagreement during an otherwise friendly program.

Although I did not agree with him, it must be acknowledged that it is the first reasonable idea that comes to mind when we attest to the power of the empire of beliefs in our contemporary world. We must differentiate two things on this point: why beliefs last *in general* and why they enjoy a strong vitality today *particularly*. Here we deal only with the second question[1]. I would like to recall some reasons which underline the counterintuitive fact that our contemporaneity encouraged the diffusion of beliefs.

This fact is first a consequence of the way in which the cognitive market has been structured historically: liberalization of supply and a huge increase in demand have brought about a whole chain of effects (increased competition, a decrease in incubation time for cognitive products, the Olson effect, the strong effect, cognitive greed, etc.).

Then, it is followed by grievances of the democratic triumvirate which relies technically in this revolution of the cognitive market (transparency, mutualization of knowledge, etc.).

At any rate, these two processes take place in an emergent way (that is to say, without being decided by anybody) as an expression of rationality's dark faces that we can synthesize with the term *democracy of the gullible*.

However, it is not advisable to try to curb this historic phenomenon. In fact, wishing to make a clean slate of the cognitive market revolution or to silence the right to expression of our fellow citizens would be both impossible and troublesome from the standpoint of the values which are the foundation of the societies that we belong to. Moreover, the cure would undoubtedly be worse than the disease. Nevertheless, if the challenge is to devise a transition between the democracy of the gullible and the democracy of enlightenment, what can be done when the former comes from processes so globalized that they cannot be confined[2]?

From an analytical point of view, this question can be conveyed to the way in which individuals cope with information. Individuals have very strong reasons to process it inadequately and to adopt beliefs that methodical reason would repeal. So, why then it cannot be imagined that educating the masses is enough? If the level of education is improved, the level of overall knowledge increases and, likewise, the level of collective gullibility mechanically decreases. This was the idea of my interlocutor, the astrophysicist; an idea as old as philosophy since it can be traced back to pre-Socratic thinkers. It is rooted on the metaphor of communicating vessels;

---

1 The former is discussed in [BRO 03] and [BRO 06].
2 An effort is made to stop these processes in China or Iran, for instance, but I am talking here about democracy.

what knowledge gains, belief would lose (and conversely). Relayed all along the history of ideas, it can be found in the pen of Montaigne, Fontenelle and even in the Encyclopedists who make of ignorance the source of every belief. This interpretation allows to dream of a society free from the excesses of gullibility. We tend to think this belief persists only in so-called backward people, in the creases of our societies, where we can find the least-learned individuals (and we think then in the peasant world mainly), but the light of education can blow away this heavy shade that has been a ballast for human destiny. Certainly, for many, it was apparent that the progress of reason was capable of creating a society where every form of superstition, of false belief, would be banished. Paul Bert declared "with science there will be no more superstition nor belief in miracles, no more coups d'Etat or revolutions". Edward Burnett Tylor, the first "institutional anthropologist" (appointed in 1896 as Chair of Anthropology in Oxford), also considered, and embodied very well the arguments upheld in those days, that history was accompanied by the development of a human spirit heading toward a growing complexity and rationality. For him, beliefs, myths and everything that separated thought from objective rationality were remnants of previous times, useful for the anthropologist who wanted to study past configurations of our cognition, but condemned to disappear from modern societies.

Therefore, proposals of this type are numerous; we can concede without discussing that the improvement of the education level, the massification of access to information and the development of science have contributed to eradicate all sorts of false ideas from public space. Thus, even if our representation of the birth of the universe is too metaphorical, it is easier for us to imagine it as the consequence of a *Big Bang* than as the separation of two colossal beings as told in the Babylonian *Enouma Elish*.

Nevertheless, a very superficial glance over our collective life shows the persistence and even the vitality of collective gullibility. But maybe this is a fact that applies to the less-educated categories of the population? In this case, Brahic and the enlightenment philosophers would be right. It would be enough to invest more in our education, especially for social categories with the lowest education level and that undoubtedly hold all types of beliefs, to continue a movement undertaken for several centuries now.

Despite all the admiration that we can hold for each other, this idea would seem questionable.

4.2. The bad education

On Monday August 25th 1835, the *New York Sun* published the first article of a series that would not go unnoticed and that was called "Great astronomical discoveries lately made by Sir John Herschel LLD, FRS & Coat the Cape of Good Hope". Until August 31st, this New York journal published the extraordinary account of the first observations of life on the moon. An account made possible by the performance of a revolutionary telescope whose technical details and assembling are thoroughly described by the articles. In the same manner, as an ethnologist observes an exotic society, John Herschel first examines the moon's vegetation. Among other things, he describes fields with red flowers resembling poppies and big needles of pale red amethyst. Soon, he is able to witness, with the help of his magnificent telescope, the existence of a fauna which is strange and familiar at the same time, herds of small-sized bisons, one-horned goats, and even better, winged men, clearly gifted with reasoning, that, according to the articles, scientists call *Vespertilio-homo*, that is "batmen"; soon, public opinion will call them "Selenites", moon inhabitants.

When this long tale was published simultaneously in the United States and France, we could have expected that the public would take it for what it was: a prank. This journalistic event is widely known now as the *moon hoax* [LAG 03]. It is difficult to assess the proportion, but it seems that many readers took this tale literally. However, what really struck the chroniclers of that time, especially the famous author Edgar Allan Poe, was that those who believed in this moon prank were not uneducated, illiterate people. They were individuals with a fair knowledge of the astronomy matters of their times and were curious about those matters.

The fact that some people with a certain level of education are not immune against the strangest beliefs can seem surprising, but this has a very general range and goes well beyond the scope of the *moon hoax*. As a matter of fact, we do not always find a link between adherence to questionable beliefs and a lack of education. Often, it is the opposite that holds true. This is what the surveys of Boy and Michelat [BOY 86], two sociologists who studied the beliefs of the French in regard to parasciences, show: "According to evidence, it is necessary to abandon a linear model in which adherence to rationalism or to scientific thinking would go hand in hand with an increase in the education level". Thus, a belief in paranormal issues or astrology first affects the non-scientific superior, then the secondary, then the superior primary and finally only the primary. Renard [REN 11] noted that middle and senior managers are statistically more faithful than workers or farmers (in regard to Unidentified Flying Object (UFOs), telepathy or even spiritism and table moving). By the same token, we can mention that those who accept more easily the myth of the Loch Ness[3] monster are also graduates; ditto for the followers of homeopathy, as Bouchayer [BOU 86] points out.

Those who launched the program *Public Understanding of Science* (PUS) in the United Kingdom, based on the notion that the concerns of public opinion about technology and science stemmed from a lack of education, ran into the same problem: there is not a linear relationship between education and one's trust in science. "Quite the contrary, resistance against technological evolution is more significant in societies with a high level of instruction. The critics of technology are far from being ignorant; they usually have a high education level" [SOL 15]. This is a fact that other inquiries have outlined. In 1979, a study, titled "The attitudes of the European public regarding scientific and technical development" [EC 79], implemented in the countries of the European Community, showed that the most educated categories are also the most critical as far as science is concerned.

There are many examples of how education does not necessarily favor a connection with scientific thought and does not make us immune against false or doubtful beliefs. Certain illustrious characters of history, reputed for their intellectual talents, were also known for their predisposition (at least relative) to bizarre beliefs. It is well known, for instance, that the president of the French Republic, François Mitterrand, considered to be an educated man with a sharp mind, used to regularly consult an astrologist. This kind of belief goes beyond political nuances; Valéry Giscard d'Estaing, Mitterrand's predecessor, also reputed for his brilliant mind, confessed on September 15th, 2001, on the *Histoire* channel, that he gave credence to astrological signs and, not less surprisingly, that he wore a fetish given to him by a Senegalese witch doctor, when he won the presidential elections in 1974[4].

---

3 According to a study led by Grimshaw and Lester quoted by J-B. Renard [REN 10].
4 Emission *Fog*, France 5, November 19 2006.

All of these facts would seem intriguing because our spontaneous interpretation of such phenomena arises more or less explicitly from a postulate that links belief and lack of education. This enigma becomes even deeper when we examine the most radical belief phenomena, like those that play a role in sectarian, religious, mystical and/or political groups. Again, contrary to what we tend to believe, it is not a lack of education that leads individuals to become fanatics. Needless to say, you can find some lunatics among extremists, and one can admit without discussion that some join radical groups because they are psychologically vulnerable or easy to manipulate. However, this type of explanation does not fully clarify a solid fact attested by all researchers who have wanted to sketch the figure of the "standard extremist". Stupple [STU 84] has shown that supporters of sectarian groups that he studied were properly integrated and balanced from a social, intellectual and moral standpoint. Likewise, Duval [DUV 02] observed, in regard to Aumism, a sect whose outrageous ideas were for a while the delight of the French Media, observed, with the support of statistical studies, that its members had not severed ties with outside society, as they read newspapers, enrolled their children in private and public schools, were members of associations, had an education level generally above the national average, etc. Sauvayre [SAU 12], in a beautiful study about individuals who decided to give up their radical beliefs, drew the same conclusions. The idea that links sectarian beliefs and a poor social and education level is plainly false. The same goes for the terrorist movements such as the IRA, the Red Brigades, the Baader-Meinhof Gang and the Japanese Red Army. This idea is also false with regard to the perpetrators of terrorist attacks on September 11th, 2001. Mohammed Atta, the kamikaze who crashed Flight 11 of American Airlines into the first tower of World Trade Center, wrote a thesis, ironically, about the rehabilitation of historic districts. We can say the same about the perpetrators of the terrorist attacks of London in July 2005, or about the islamist cell in Montpellier, dismantled in March 2006, and that was integrated by French students of Moroccan origin, coming from well-off backgrounds, sometimes of mixed parentage and pursuing engineering studies at the *Université de Sciences et Techniques* in Languedoc (Montpellier II). Generally speaking, we can see that most perpetrators of attacks had advanced degrees and came from well-off backgrounds, as Cohen points out [COH 02]. Studies of Islamic terrorism led toward the same diagnostic. In this way, Sageman [SAG 04] undertook a rigorous study about the general characteristics of Al-Qaïda terrorists and found that most do not come from the deprived or working class backgrounds. This was also observed by Khosrokhavar [KHO 06, p. 318]: "The myth of the community unified by the allegiance to Allah does not preclude the unity of the proletariat under the guidance of a self-proclaimed avant-garde that, as we know, was made up of middle-class individuals often with a high education, as with the contemporary islamist phenomenon". This is corroborated by Etienne [ETI 05] in his study *Les combattants suicidaires (Suicide Fighters)*, Krueger [KRU 07] in *Ce qui fait un terroriste (What makes a terrorist)*, Crenshaw in his article "The causes of terrorism" or Ruby [RUB 02] in a text where he wonders "if terrorists are mentally deranged".

4.3. When gullibility looks like intelligence

When Edgar Allan Poe became interested in the *moon hoax*, what surprised him the most was that "those who had doubts were not able to explain why. They were ignorant; they had no idea about astronomy, people who could not believe because those things were too new, too distant from common knowledge". Even as surprised as he was, Poe gives us a very interesting initial clue to interpret this fact. Why were the most educated people the ones who bought this hoax more easily? Undoubtedly, he thought, it is because their education favored a certain *mental disposition*, a way of expanding their intellectual horizon. Those with an interest in astronomy were aware that other planets exist, knew that the Earth was not the center of the universe and that life had the potential to exist elsewhere. Victims of the moon hoax, therefore, had some reasons to believe in it (though they were not right to believe). This cognitive method is properly illustrated by the metaphor of Pascal's sphere. If knowledge is a sphere, Pascal explains, its surface is in contact with what it does not contain, in other words, the unknown. Hence, when knowledge spreads, as does the surface of the sphere, the air in contact with ignorance does not stop spreading either. In fact, it is not ignorance that grows symmetrically with knowledge, but the awareness of that which is unknown, that is to say, the awareness of the lack of information that characterizes our grasp of certain matters. This awareness can be perfectly placed at the service of gullibility.

What better example than remembering the ambitions of spiritism, the belief that met a phenomenal success at the turn of the 19th and 20th Centuries and that pretended to prove that it was possible to get in touch with the dead? Flammarion, a scientist by training and a big supporter of this doctrine, gave a speech of exemplary clarity during the funerals of Allan Kardec[5], on April 2nd 1869: "Spiritism is not a religion, but a science, and we only know the ABC of this science". The ambition that Flammarion had for spiritism was precisely based on the argument about the widening of science conceptions. He insisted on the incomplete nature of human knowledge, and he stressed that spiritual matters could be compared with electric phenomena, bright and caloric and still poorly understood. The latest scientific and technical findings, beginning with electromagnetic waves and the wireless telegraph that uses such waves, would demonstrate, in his view, that a remote action was possible, and, therefore, that certain dimensions of our universe eluded our senses: "The physical sciences teach us that we live in the middle of a world that is invisible to us, and that it is not impossible that some beings (equally invisible to us) live also on Earth, in an order of sensations that is absolutely different to ours; we don't have the ability to perceive their presence, unless they manifest by events that emerge in our order of sensations" [FUE 02]. In other words, according to Flammarion, the concepts proclaimed by the spiritism doctrine are actually plausible in the light of scientific findings; and it is not inconceivable that our universe is also inhabited by beings that the ordinary man cannot perceive, on account of their immateriality. This argument clashed, in the cognitive market, against the position of those who maintained that metaphysical phenomena are impossible and, as a result, spiritual beliefs are false. Yet, since "rationalist" spirits can make a deduction of the type: *A is impossible, therefore A is false*, why, supporters of spiritism ask, one cannot respond: *A is possible therefore A is true?* Many did not see that the logical symmetry of this answer does not confer it the status of a solid argument at all, and they took it, therefore, as a good reason to believe in a metaphysical reality. This paralogism is what makes many beliefs compatible with our contemporaneity. Apparently, its seductive powers work better when aiming at spirits that have enjoyed some sort of intellectual training. This holds especially true when this learning is only superficial, like in the case of scientific disciplines in higher education courses of literature or human and social sciences. This reasoning can be helpful to better understand the results obtained by Boy and Michelat in their inquiry about the beliefs of the French with regard to parasciences. Being familiar with the history of sciences (and with "the non-scientific superior stage" more than "the secondary stage") allows us to imagine that a scientific system is a grid, temporary most of the time, which is never totally in line with reality. These students are, therefore, familiar with the controversial side

---

5 Allan Kardec (Hippolyte Léon Denizard Rivail) is the founder of spiritism.

of science which is not necessarily apparent for an individual who only has elementary studies. However, for those who have reached the *scientific* superior stage, fidelity to certain beliefs becomes more difficult because this contradicts a system of representation inherited from the comprehensive study of the laws that rule exact sciences. This makes their belief in the paranormal remarkably similar to that of primary school students who have not received any significant scientific training. Likewise, the scientific superior clearly separates from the rest with regard to a belief in astrology: this one implies more than a planetary influence over individuals, it is deemed as some sort of divination; therefore, it is even more difficult, when compared with the paranormal, to reconcile this practice with a sharp knowledge in the field of exact sciences.

Studies should refine a critical spirit if we believe in the ambitions of diverse thinkers who have inspired the pedagogical programs of our college and high-school students. Many of the exercises that clutter our pedagogical path attempt to find the sense camouflaged behind appearances. What is the unfathomable meaning of this literary piece, of this poem? What intentions and issues are masked in this historic document? Our children are taught with all kinds of hermeneutical practices, and are encouraged to find the hidden meaning of things to express their intelligence. Soon, they will come across the thinking of Freud, Nietzsche and Marx, the great philosophers of suspicion, and, at university, Bourdieu, constructivism, culturalism, relativism, etc. Undoubtedly, these are very useful exercises for the formation of reason; however, as a hypothesis, I suppose that the scientific representation of the world can also pay a price. These exercises certainly bring up the idea that those things that we hold as true can, at best, compete with other ways of seeing, or, even worse, can be considered as illusions. As an example, what can we think of that which a manual of sociology of sciences proposes to students as an exercise and above all, what can we think of its vision statement[6]?

> "To evaluate the extension of a scientific conviction, for instance, that according to which "$U = R.I$". To wander through different social spaces and see where this belief spreads, and if it is the same everywhere: see also

---

6 I take this example from the Alexandre Moatti's blog, available at: http://www.maths-et-physique.net/article-croyez-vous-en-la-loi-d-ohm-103035280.html.

fundamentalist physicists, Engineers working for EDF, neighborhood electricians and students".

It is clearly mentioned that they call it "belief", and the term "fundamentalist" physicists says a lot about the way in which a certain discourse that considers itself critical thinking has been able to boost the democracy of the gullible. There is a huge jump between the perfectly acceptable idea that we must not consider that everything that science declares is written in stone, and to consider that scientific propositions are beliefs just like any other. This slippery logic of relativism[7] is nothing fatal, and there are many minds that are opposed. However, there are many who let themselves be taken and find astrologic, paranormal and homeopathic hypotheses alluring, not only because of the services that they render to every mind who wants to feel reassured, but rather because they are based on false arguments, pseudo-evidence that we could consider at odds with scientific propositions, once we admit that the latter could not benefit from any argument of authority (which is more easily admitted by individuals with an education than by those without any). In the same way, the arguments of the precautionist militants are considered as legitimate (and much more accepted by the journalist and public opinion in many cases) than those held by orthodox science. It is ironic to see that one of the figure heads of contemporary relativism Bruno Latour seems to be changing his mind. In his book, *Enquête sur les modes d'existence (Inquiry about Lifestyles)*, he shows concern about the fact that climate risks are not always taken seriously. After all, why should we rely on the benefits of science on this matter but not on that of the GMO or frequent low waves? Latour does not answer this embarrassing question, but, since he shows concern about climate, he finds his fight against the institution a lot less amusing. He confesses with a rather puzzling naivety: "At first, the fight against the institution did not seem dangerous; it was modernizing and liberating, even amusing. Just like asbestos, it had nothing but good qualities. Alas, just like asbestos, it had devastating consequences that nobody anticipated and that we were too slow to recognize"[8].

Furthermore, these beliefs that we often talk about require a culture or *subculture* that is not within everyone's reach. Arguments that support these beliefs are sometimes subtle and technical; which gives them an air of truth and ultimately of science, as we have seen; and can only exert their attraction

---

7 I do not have the space to start an argument against relativism. In this respect, see [BOU 94] and [BOU 08].
8 Quoted in "Who's afraid of scientific truths?", *Le Monde*, 22/09/12.

on minds prepared to receive them. Frequently, it is more difficult to convince these citizens of the democracy of the gullible when they are persuaded that they are properly informed about a determined subject. Thus, we understand more clearly the results mentioned at the introduction of this book regarding the distrust of individuals about nuclear matters or GMO (58% declare that they do not trust scientists to tell the truth about GMO or nuclear matters), while they relatively trust them with regard to neurosciences (only 25% declare that they do not trust them). The aforementioned study[9] also shows that among those who answered the survey, 71% think that they do not have a clear understanding of neuroscience, while 63 and 67% believe they have a firm grasp on matters of GMO and nuclear issues. In other words, the more they think they know a subject, the more they question the scientist.

Again, the development of the Internet accompanies and prolongs this movement, as some people are persuaded that they can find the information that has been hidden from us online. Thus, those who obtained a high degree in France are the least likely to believe the information seen on television; however, they are the most likely to believe what appears on the Internet; 45% of those graduates find the Internet information perfectly reliable, as compared with only 11% of those who did not graduate[10].

Moreover, as a token of the Internet culture, *Wikipedia* puts into practice a definition of truth that we could call polyphonical [CAR 10, p. 88]: when several interpretations of the same phenomenon are possible, the online encyclopedia shows all the different interpretations in a balanced manner. Many will find that this way of producing information is commendable, but it also leads to a form of relativism because it places all contributors on equal footing, regardless of their level of expertise. After all, is it not arguments that count the most, and not diplomas? The problem, as we have seen it throughout this book, is that every half-scholar can present a convincing argument about almost every single subject, with sources that would seem as honorable as any other. *Wikipedia* is a terrific tool (I must confess I use it quite often) but, at the same time, this democratic procedure of pooling information leads to abuses that favor the democracy of the gullible. The issue of medical knowledge is, for instance, a sensitive one, as we find some orthodox knowledge, as well as propositions arising from pseudo sciences, folk knowledge and other superstitions circumstantially named

---

9 See http://www.larecherche.fr/content/system/media/Rapport.pdf.
10 See http://www.tns-sofres.com/_assets/files/2011.02.08-baro-media.pdf.

"unconventional medicine". This effort to achieve equality by ignoring the skill levels of the various contributors is a feature that we will never find in a traditional encyclopedia since its intention is, precisely, anti-relativistic. The spirit of enlightenment seems to vanish in the horizon and the situation does bear some resemblance to certain parts of Plato's Phaedrus: "Science is an illusion, not reality; when they actually be able to obtain, without learning, plenty of information, they will consider themselves well-versed in a variety of things when in fact most of them are incompetent, insufferable in their trade, because instead of being scholars, they will become illusion scholars!"

4.4. The sum of imperfections

It would be absurd to defend the idea that education is harmful for the diffusion of knowledge. What I have tried to emphasize is that in order to go from a democracy of the gullible to a democracy of enlightenment (on the understanding that these are *typical* forms and there is a *continuum* between them), the solution is not to increase the general education level of a population, for there is not a distinct correlation between level of education and an insightful view of the world[11].

Therefore, since we cannot nor should we want to limit the perverse effects of the cognitive market revolution by boxing it through a political voluntarism that could become dictatorial, the solution is to be found right at the center of our minds.

Let us start by stressing that every education effort that democratic societies have undertaken seems to have forgotten a key issue of knowledge: if critical thinking is exercised without a method, it will easily lead to gullibility. Doubt has heuristic virtues, that much is true, but it can lead, instead of mental autonomy, to cognitive nihilism.

Science comes precisely from the examination of that version of reality offered by our senses and our ordinary logic, but the essential of this procedure lies in the way it reconstructs a vision of the world: it does so with a method. For those who demand the *right to doubt*, such as the interlocutor I quoted in the introduction of this book, it responds: "Yes, but every right carries with it a duty". I see then in our education system the honorable and omnipresent will to develop one form of intellectual autonomy throughout

---

11 However, we can find a relation between the education level and the endorsement of certain beliefs (notably, conspirationist).

doubt, but I see very little of that which I think is the cornerstone of every pedagogy: the teaching of the method. What relativists do not seem to notice is that the methods used in science that took thousands of years to emerge, after some hesitations, mistakes and drastic selections, are a universal heritage. They are not a typically western thing, nor are they the expression of a classist culture even if history shows certain decisive instants of the definition of this method in appearing this or that place. We can easily demonstrate that a specific scientist played a role in a social area, that he held religious beliefs, that he had ideological obsessions, interests and that all those things possibly molded his hypothesis; furthermore, in the worst-case scenario, he could have discovered the truth with some very specific intentions that other scientists would not find commendable. To put the biography of every scientist under the "microscope" can generate a plethora of hypotheses with regard to the social nature of the theories they have created. This exercise could lead to missing the essential point, which is that the scholar's proposition, his experiment protocol and his results will be evaluated by individuals who also carry their interests and beliefs, but not necessarily the same ones. Time will subject these propositions to the filter of the most demanding Darwinian selection that has been used in the history of human kind. This does not mean that this selection is enough to find nothing but the truth, yet, reason wants us to put our epistemic trust in this mode of selecting cognitive proposals rather than any other, claiming for democracy. What history has shown us is that scientific thinking can be seen, typically, as an effort made to surpass the universal limits of human rationality that keep us from being omniscient subjects and turn us mechanically into faithful subjects. As I see it, those limits are of three types[12].

First, our mind is dimensionally limited because our conscience is locked up in a restricted space and an everlasting present. Furthermore, it is culturally limited for it interprets every information in terms of preconceived representations. Finally, it is ballasted from a cognitive standpoint because our ability to process information is not infinite and the complexity of certain problems exceeds the potentiality of our common sense.

These three limits are probably insurmountable. Indeed, an individual in his natural state, assuming he is not a god, cannot know beyond time and space, or by ignoring the cultural and cognitive transfer of information.

---

12 Undoubtedly, it will be necessary to add the pollution of belief by desire and emotion.

Nevertheless, he can expect to reduce the harming power of these limits of rationality and try to go beyond his egocentric perceptions of the world. This kind of effort characterizes the great milestones of human knowledge. We can try, as an exercise, to describe some important stages in the progress of knowledge as the result of a historic movement to wipe out these three flaws of our understanding. It is an exercise that I am not capable of undertaking, but I will propose some of the most popular examples drawn from the history of sciences in order to give some substance to this idea.

Let us go back to the first limit of rationality, the one linked to our dimensional condition. Our conception of space has significantly evolved. Gradually, we have given up the beliefs that the Earth (the space we share) is flat (Parmenides already advocated the idea of the spherical shape), that it is the center of the universe (Aristarchus of Samos proposed the hypothesis of Earth rotating around the sun, and not the opposite) and that it is motionless (Heraclides Ponticus suggested that the Earth rotated around itself).

All these conceptions that were offered in the cognitive market took a long time to impose. Thus, the heliocentric system was conceived, albeit in a less sophisticated version, 18 centuries before Copernicus. The fact that this system took longer to establish itself in human thinking than the geocentric system has many elaborate explanations, but no explanation can disqualify the idea that this late acceptance is mostly due to the fact that it is counter-intuitive; to show its superiority, it had to overcome the feeling of immediate and deceiving evidence that is recognized by the spatial limits of our understanding. It is true; in fact, this ordinary observation leads us to believe that the sun rotates around the Earth, and not the other way around.

More generally, we also know that space is no longer a simple container as we are told by our senses and our experience, for physical facts like gravitation can alter it.

We know that time does not follow a straight line and that it can also be deformed; the way it deploys depends on the reference system considered.

In conclusion, we have learned to go beyond the notion that time and space *as seen* are the standard measure of nature's phenomena; in other words, we have learned to mistrust the information that comes to us in the limit of our senses and therefore, to "decontextualize" the rationality of its dimensional environment.

Nevertheless, the *whole* of the knowledge is less than the sum of its parts. It is stunning to note that nowadays many people still believe that the sun rotates around the Earth and not the other way around. This distancing of the limits of our rationality is never a collective and definitive experience; it is an effort that common sense can accept, but it is more typical of the scientific approach.

Certain physical data are systematically comprised "chronologically" even if they take place simultaneously, which becomes difficult for our time-oriented reasoning; thus, as Viennot [VIE 96] stresses in his works about the way common sense perceives physics, the notorious ideal gas equation imposes a conception of simultaneity, with constant pressure, for variations of volume and temperature, which is a torment for ordinary reasoning.

What has just been briefly mentioned about the dimensional character of our self-centered thinking could be more telling with regard to the second category of limits for our rationality.

History of knowledge was rather late to take seriously the idea that our culture could subject reality to the bed of Procust. It is a fact that the people have a certain inclination to ethnocentrism, that is to say, to consider that their culture is an exact translation of reality and should, therefore, be above the rest. It was necessary to wait, in part, the anthropology of the 20th Century and a self-analysis of Western Culture to methodically undertake this detachment with the cultural limits of our thinking. The method "participant observation" defended and implemented by Bronislaw Malinowski, and Claude Lévi-Strauss manifest, *Race and history*, propose two typical examples of attempts to take a distance from cultural limits of rationality. This exercise can, in addition, lead to excesses; relativism is one illustration, for it inspires the hyperbolic idea that systems of representation, being cultural constructions, could not be easily distinguished from each other from a point of view of the *real*.

The notion that our culture guides our perception and our understanding is not new at all; tradition usually traces it back to Bacon and to the clear awareness he had of the need to overcome the sociocultural prism to achieve an objective mode of knowledge.

The third category of limits that undermine our rationality and that is fundamental for the triumph of the democracy of the gullible is the one related to the cognitive mistakes that we discussed with some examples throughout this book. It has also given rise to a heap of reflections that pervade the history of human thinking. We can find many who pioneered a great deal of the research about the cognitive limits of reality [BRO 07a]. In this, a special place should be reserved for John Stuart Mill and his *A System of Logic*, to Vilfredo Pareto ... but, to tell the truth, all these contributions only anticipated the research led by two psychologists, Amos Tversky and Daniel Kahnemanlate, in the 20th Century. They prepared a cartography of reasoning errors based on experimental data that has yet to meet its match[13].

If we take a quick look at the scientific methods in practical terms, i.e. epimediological approach, double-blind protocol required, etc., we will see attempts to "filter out " the constraints of rationality, and due to that, they achieve their universal dimension. The scientist inherits, through his professional practice, a method to apprehend reality which is more efficient than that of others. There remains a man, however, he is not immune to the damaging effects of these rational limits, who carries within himself as a cognitive Scrooge waiting for his time to come, just as much as the man of interest, either economic or ideological; that is why the propositions that he will make in the cognitive market should always go through the inquisitive filter of his pairs, who give a collective dimension to this. When insisting in a deconstruction of scientific knowledge, critical and relativist thinking unweaves a piece of fabric and is then astonished when it only finds an empty space. With this approach, it misses the possibility of understanding that the sum of imperfections can lead to principles of universal scope. However, such principles will never find more trouble than when going against the natural propensities of our minds; yet, this is the place when they are most useful.

For a long time, this reality was not obnoxious insofar as the expertise clarified the political decision, detached somehow from ordinary logic. However, deregulation of the cognitive market helped ordinary logic to invite itself to the table of discussions. I find that this situation is an important moment in the history of democracies and irreversible as well. Yet, our education systems and certain relativist ideology have prepared us better to undo knowledge rather than to redo it; more participation in the debate could help to amplify the phenomenon of mistake mutualization that can already be observed.

---

13 For a collective and temporary summary of these works, see [TVE 84b].

4.5. Toward cognitive demagogy

For demagogy, the classical dictionary definition is: "A policy, through which one cajoles, excites, exploits the passions of the masses" (*Dictionary Le Robert*). The discourse defined in this way seeks to flatter the natural propensities of the interlocutor's mind. Most of the time, those who invoke this term insist on the emotional tone (anger, jingoism and hatred of the other) of the discourse. However, it is a form of demagogy that leans on hollow arguments (which can be complementary to an expression of emotion rather than to some irrepressible affective reflexes)[14].

Let us take the renowned example of propaganda, such as the slogan of Nazi ideologues: "Three million unemployed, three million Jews". This parallelism of numbers must always accompany a simplistic explanation that tries to grab the attention of certain public; yet, it also arises from the fact that this explanation tries to tamper with (deliberately) the confusion between correlation and causality. Political ideologies (especially the extremist) love to take advantage of the penchant which we have to believe that a co-occurrence is forcefully the sign, even the proof, of a causal relationship.

Again, we cannot say that this argument is objectively rational, but we miss the heart of the matter if we do not see that it pulls its strength from an inferential process, certainly wrong, but which is the expression of some kind of limited rationality.

It turns out that certain silly and/or heinous ideas will triumph, prevail and sometimes be more successful than other more reasonable and balanced ideas, because they will capitalize on this inferential process, questionable but appealing to the mind. Thus, this situation has become even more dangerous now that we witness this deregulation of the cognitive market made tangible by the increased competition between conventional media and, especially, by the emergence of the Internet. Formerly, those whom the theory of communication called gate *keepers* (journalists, expert commentators, etc.) made sure, for better or worse, that certain ideas could

---

14 The old opposition reason/emotion has lost a lot of its appeal since brain sciences have shown how these two mental realities can be intertwined.

not easily be spread. Today, these have seriously weakened … again, for better or worse.

Better, we all know, are the terrific collaborating work exercises proposed by the Internet. For instance, the game *Foldit* asks the Internet users to attempt molecular combinations to get a better understanding of the way proteins can deploy in space: the point is to remove fragments here, to add them there or even to destroy some bonds. This collective game of construction has led to the publication of three articles, one of them in the renowned magazine *Nature*.

Worse still is the propagation of a variety of cognitive demagoguery that wants to impose, little by little, the intuitive points of view, sometimes mistaken, in all kinds of subjects, regardless of whether this is about perception of technological risks or conspiracy theories.

If we take the example of technological risks, at a time when health and environment alerts have become overwhelming, we must remember that the functioning of the human mind favors the diffusion of fears and worries, even if they are not always well founded. It turns out that we are poorly equipped to rationally assess this kind of situation. For instance, we perceive low probabilities as being much more likely to happen than they actually are.

Public debates focus on high-voltage antennas, relay antennas, nuclear energy, GMOs, etc.; we admit that risks are unlikely. However, we never do it without exposing the scenarios where the unlikely takes place and, hence, without eliciting a disposition shared by many minds to overvalue low probabilities. Televised or radio debates give a pretty good idea of the way debates entrench on these presumed low possibilities (they are rarely backed up with real figures, but we assume they are not zero). Yet, for many decades now, psychology has shown that we tend to misrepresent probabilities when they are low. These results have been confirmed and refined, especially by Prelec [PRE 98]. When these probabilities are low (1 in 10,000 and less) on average, they are perceived 10–15 times higher by the common man. In the same way, high probabilities (0.98–0.99) tend to be considerably underestimated.

This subjective representation of probabilities gave rise to advanced formulations that led to establish the following curve.

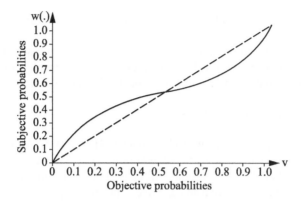

Figure 4.1. *Curve of subjective probabilities*

This graph presents objective probabilities (v) on the x-axis and probabilities as perceived by ordinary logic (w) on the y-axis. If individuals had a perfect representation of probabilities, the relation between v and w would be described by a proportional line. This is not the case, as we can see, the closeness to value 0 (that is to say, low probabilities) creates a brief but dramatic distortion. This cognitive bias of human reason can bear important implications in a deregulated market. As a matter of fact, the information supplier who attaches himself more or less blindly to the demand will progressively lean toward a demagogical representation of risk. Moreover, we should add many other mental illusions that weigh on our minds: we give more consideration to the costs than to the benefits of a given situation; we easily give up to an appetite for zero risk and prefer to avoid choices before uncertainty. We always give more consideration to the costs than to the benefits. The Nobel Economy Award winner, Daniel Kahneman [TVE 86], highlighted in his works that to psychologically compensate a cost of 1 euro, a profit of 2.50 euros is needed. We can also remember that we are more afraid of the consequences brought about by our actions than those brought about by our inaction. All these considerations show why the Internet, because it flirts with cognitive demagogy, promotes the diffusion of collective fears which can turn into a demand for a moratorium on the diffusion of such and such technological innovation.

Everything that is part of the oldest ways of thinking will enjoy a new visibility and legitimacy due to this deregulation of the information market.

4.6. How to keep the illusion scholar inside us in check

Since reversing the cognitive limits of rationality is an essential requisite to conceive a transition toward a democracy of enlightenment, at this moment of the book, I have two pieces of news, one good and one bad.

Let us start with the bad news.

The philosopher Jonathan Cohen [COH 81] from Oxford University wondered whether it would be possible to bring to zero the existence of those systematic and predictable reasoning mistakes. In his opinion, they arose from education deficiencies more than cognitive deficiencies. The problem is that, in an article prior to the text of Cohen (since it dates back to 1971), Tversky and Kahneman had already demonstrated that statistical experts could make cognitive blunders just like those made by the common man. They recount an experience they had while attending a colloquy sponsored by the group of mathematical psychology and the American Association of Psychology. They asked 84 individuals who attended this meeting to answer the following question: "If you know that a set of twenty subjects has confirmed your theory, what is the likelihood, in your opinion, that an additional group of ten persons confirm your story separately?" Only nine people gave answers ranging between 0.4 and 0.6. Most gave estimations close to 0.85. The first answer is of course more reasonable, which suggests that familiarity with formal logic and the theory of probabilities do not prevent mistaken intuitions.

Another example, more spectacular and with potentially severe consequences, was told by Casscells *et al.* [CAS 78] who posed a question to 60 students and professors from Harvard's School of Medicine; it went like this:

> *A disease that affects one person out of a thousand can be detected by a test. This test has a rate of positive errors of 5%; that is to say, the rate of false positives is 5%. One individual undergoes the test. The result is positive. What are the probabilities it is right?*

We would not expect that medics be totally unfamiliar with this kind of problem; yet, they were massively mistaken on this subject. Thus, the majority answered: 95% (the average of all answers was 56%). In fact, only 18% of medics and medical trainees gave the right answer: 2%.

As a matter of fact, "5% of false positives" means that out of 100 healthy individuals, 5 individuals test positive. Therefore, the reasoning goes as follows: out of 100,000, 99,900 are healthy and 4,995 are false positives. Meanwhile, only 100 were actually sick.

Thus,

$$100/(100 + 4995) = 100/5095 \approx 2$$

In this case, if even statisticians and medics, used to dealing with probabilistic questions, make significant mistakes, what can be expected non-trained from individuals? The problem brought up by these mental illusions is not really a matter of education level, but actually of cognition. However, I do not think that the question made by Cohen is useless. Indeed, if the level of education is not a definitive protection against cognitive mistakes, is it possible, by means of any given intellectual formation, to tame them?

And this is the good news: yes, it is possible to weaken the power of attraction that this strange reasoning exerts on our minds.

If we go back to the issue of the medical test, it can be shown that posing the same question in a different manner, the error rate literally plummets:

Among 1,000 individuals, one finds that, on average, one is affected by disease X. For every thousand healthy Americans, one finds 50 persons, on average, that test positive. Imagine that we choose 1,000 Americans randomly, how many, among those who tested positive, have actually contracted the disease?

In this form, 76% of individuals got the right answer (as compared with 18% with the previous wording)[15]. The fearful confirmation bias that Wason implemented experimentally (see section 1.3.1) could also be inhibited in a spectacular manner, as developmental psychologist Olivier Houdé and his team showed it [HOU 00].

Even if this is an alluring subject, I will put aside the question of knowing where those biases come from: are they a biological legacy of our distant past, or, on the contrary, do we acquire them when our brain is developing[16]? In any event, these biases, in most cases, are not so uprooted in us that it

---

15 See [COS 96] or [GIG 09] who has worked with the same type of wording with German medics.
16 It is a question that was of considerable interest for me, especially in [BRO 07a].

becomes impossible to reduce their damaging power on our mental life or on the resulting collective processes. This, in the end, gives rise to certain optimism, and anticipates a vast undertaking that I just reviewed here. I think this undertaking could take at least three forms: the first form affects our education system, the second form, a type of communication engineering, notably scientific, which takes into account the dark side of our rationality to allow a better communication; and the third form calls for the emergence of a new form of militancy.

4.7. Declaration of mental independence

Suppose that you are a juror in an especially sensitive trial. Three months ago, a man died, run over accidentally by a hit-and-run taxi. In this city, there are only blue taxis and green taxis (85% of green taxis and 15% of blue taxis). In the course of the trial, a witness shows up. The event took place at night and we can suspect that the witness, who allegedly saw a blue cab, could be wrong. Some visual tests are prepared to assess his statement. It is found that in the night condition, he was able to recognize a blue taxi in 80% of the instances. This testimony is paramount, for, if he properly identified the color of the taxi, then the individual under investigation is guilty. In your opinion, what is the percentage chance that this driver, who has a blue taxi, is responsible for this accident?

When the question is asked, most individuals questioned were wrong when answering 80%. Doesn't this remind you of something? This problem bears some resemblance to the one we just saw in the previous section about the medical test. As a matter of fact, it hides the same cognitive structure[17]: just like the medical test, where we tended to overlook the structure of the population, sick or healthy, we simply act as if the answer was independent of the rate of blue and green taxis. Maybe, you did not find the right answer which is 41% (it is not at all the same thing as 80% when we place a guilty bet involving the fate of a man), but surely you had a déjà vu feeling that made you distrust this statement. You were on guard. That is reassuring.

By contrast, if you had been asked about the taxi problem 1 month after the question of the medical tests, surely you would have made the same mistake without any kind of mistrust: this is discouraging. A *trace* of cognitive bias remains. To fight against this persistence, it is not enough to imagine, once and for all, the problem and its solution, especially since

---

17 That of *Neglect of the basic rate* [TVE 84].

cognitive biases, as those two problems show, have many shapes, especially when they emerge in a social context. To foresee one of its forms does not guarantee that we can resist them permanently. It is important to rethink the way in which our education system could help young minds to break free, better than we were able to, from this bias that hampers a fair perception of things.

This is how, despite the generalized increase in the level of education and scientific culture of the population in democratic societies, many perception errors remain in our representation of the world. Several surveys show that 30% of Europeans think that it is the Sun that turns around the Earth and not the other way around[18]. Morel [MOR 02, p. 121] also noted that educated people, with advanced degrees, believe that the moon phases are the result of the shadow that Earth projects over its natural satellite. Yet, these persons learned very well at school that the Earth does revolve around the Sun and not the other way around, but since the perception of our senses easily displaces those teachings, some fall prey to this false impression. Things would be very different if the lesson they received would have taken into account how difficult would it be to remember this in the future. In other words, if this astronomy lesson was accompanied by a guiding light over the cognitive hurdles that hamper its good reception. Education cannot make the deceiving suggestion of our eyes disappear, but it can sharpen a reflex of impatience. We will always feel this mental temptation to perceive the world in an egocentric manner, but our education can help us to fight it with a more methodical vision. The latter is more expensive (in terms of time and mental energy). We cannot, therefore, make use of it for every purpose at all times (cognitive greed, as we have seen, is necessary for life in society and for our individual survival). By contrast, it is possible to conceive a way of learning that helps us recognize the cognitive situations where we must suspend our judgment and our sometimes deceiving intuitions.

In this respect, a fine study by Shtulman and Valcarcel [SHT 12] shows that certain propositions are less well accepted than others. Their project consisted of asking individuals 200 questions that spanned six different scientific subjects (astronomy, genetics, thermodynamics, etc.); they had to

---

18 A survey carried out in the European Union between May 10th and June 15th 2001 shows that 26.1% of respondents think that the sun revolves around the Earth and 7.1% confess that they do not know. This opinion poll commissioned by the Joint Research Center was carried out throughout all the states that were members of the European Union in 2001.

respond "true" or "false" to statements like: "The moon generates light"; "1/13 is bigger than 1/30"; "Atoms are essentially void". The participants had known at one time or another of their intellectual journey, the answers to those questions and should have *known* rather than believed. The results of the study show that the mistake is never bigger than when there is a conflict between our intuitions of the world and the propositions of science. Even when respondents are not wrong, they take more time to answer. Time in this case is a good indication of what costs to us, in terms of mental energy, the struggle against the fundamental limits of rationality. To continue our reflection, we can notice that an early acquaintance with scientific culture does not totally preclude deceiving intuitions but can inhibit them remarkably.

It turns out that we begin to know the map of our systematic errors very well. It is, no doubt, still incomplete, but it would permit us to improve our ways of learning without giving up the quality of the content. Some will say that is like reinventing the wheel and that some things are set in stone. All those who, like me, know the statistics, know very well that a moment must be reserved to explain to students that there should be no confusion between correlation and causality (*it is not because two events take place at the same time, that one is the result of the other*). But, they also know that students do not begin to develop a reflex of mistrust unless they engage in repeated exercises. Those that can compete against this mistake will pave the way in human thinking. These mental illusions can emerge in every field of knowledge: physics, biology, mathematics, economic and social sciences, history, philosophy, etc. In fact, pedagogical programs are full of it; pedagogues have not noticed or taken it seriously. I, for instance, led an investigation [BRO 07b] to assess the way individuals (all Baccalaureate holders) understood the theory of evolution. The result was undisputed; for the vast majority defended the finalist theories[19] rather than the Darwinian thesis. It was not because of ideological or religious reasons (many believed that the solution they proposed had Darwinian bases) as can be seen in the United States, but simply because mechanisms described by the theory of evolution clash with cognitive obstacles that make it counterintuitive[20]. The only way of effectively teaching this theory, so paramount to our understanding of the world (and to prevent certain religious interpretations of

---

19 Finalist theses affirm, for instance, that if giraffes have a long neck, it is because they can go find food at the top of the tress (function creates the organ). The Darwinian thesis affirms that among giraffes, those with a long neck, survived more easily, bred and little-by-little became the "normal" giraffe population.
20 In this case, *the omission in the sample's size.*

the kind: God does things the right way or, a more current variation, Nature does things the right way), is to insist through a series of repeated exercises, on the mechanisms that control it. Even worse, I rescheduled the experiment[21], under the same conditions, but this time with 56 professors of natural and life sciences, from middle school and high school. It turns out that one of two evoked finalist theses and found them credible. The interviews with these professors are often fascinating for they show that they obviously know the theory of evolution (they begin usually by giving a lesson about the subject so that the sociologist "stays in his place"), but when the time comes to apply it in a concrete case, they do not resist the temptation represented by the finalist thesis.

The issue is not only about understanding Darwin's theory, but also about breaking free from mental temptations that take part in many expressions of collective gullibility. Indeed, the cognitive processes involved here demonstrate our common difficulty to understand the processes, sometimes lengthy, of reciprocal selection and adjustment that arise from natural or social phenomena. When dealing with natural phenomena, the beliefs involved are finalist and often, in an implicit or explicit manner, religious. When it comes to social phenomena, we assume that some hidden intentions exist behind complex events or aggregations of actions by individuals who have no idea whatsoever of the results they are going to produce; we have to wonder in this case; who benefits from the crime? Thus, we get very close to going from a critical thinking to a conspirational thinking. This is how they make up domination theories that are shamelessly defended by those who could poke fun at this kind of explanation with regard to natural phenomena, but they find these theories ingenious when it comes to social phenomena; gullibility that poses as intelligence. If those cognitive biases can easily contaminate some minds that otherwise can be brilliant, it is because they allow their concept of the good to contaminate their conception of the truth (for having a metaphysical or ideological interpretation of the world), as well as because they have not learned to recognize the expression of those biases in different problem structures. They are rationalist here and gullible there.

What I will call the *real critical mind*, that is to say, that which is going to help us to counter the alienation that is sometimes represented by the suggestions of our intuition, can only be acquired through constant exercises.

---

21 Results not yet published and obtained with the help from the students of Paris IV and those from the interannual survey of l'*Université de Strasbourg* whom I thank here.

For this reason, the work discussed in this book is essential to create a democracy of enlightenment that can only be done by insisting throughout the education phase, in all subjects, as soon as is reasonably possible. It is important to emphasize methodical thinking to encourage individuals to be critical of their own intuitions, to identify the situations where one's own judgment must be put on hold, to invest energy and time instead of accepting a solution that seems acceptable; in one word, to control the cognitive Scrooge that lives inside all of us. To teach anything one must be effective and take into account and the characteristics of the receiver of the message. These characteristics may be common and invariant, but they cannot be overlooked by learning. If the process of democratization of democracy is well underway, and since it would be difficult to disagree, the demands of the democratic *triumvirate* are going to become increasingly pressing. I find it less utopian than necessary to get ready for this pedagogical revolution, the one that will lead us to pronounce our mental declaration of independence.

4.8. The fourth power

This effort for the formation of the minds must be particularly conceived for those whose profession is to disseminate information. We think especially of journalists; we have already seen that they can play an important role in the democracy of the gullible. These are individuals just like the rest of us and can easily indulge on mental illusions and on their ideological prisms, as they face the urgent need to submit information. I do not think it is outrageous to ask, however, if they could be a little bit above the rest of men, because of their paramount role in democracies.

As we have seen, journalists are often trapped in a situation called the prisoner's dilemma. However, if in journalism schools, and likewise in all the places where they educate those who are going to comment on information, students were made aware of those cognitive biases, of what we know of social stereotypes or if they could get a good grasp of urban legends, the future professionals could develop the mistrust reflex so necessary in situations where they are competing for the information. This mistrust, I remind you, is aimed at one's self and at the performance of one's own reasoning: to be able, against the evidence of one's intuition, to generate inside the laboratory of the conscience, methodical, alternative hypotheses.

Thus, a story about some unpleasant officials in a provincial town, who organize satanic and pedophile networks, should elicit mistrust in those who are initiated to the typical material of urban legends. The same goes for the apparition of a spider or a small snake in the fruit and vegetable section of a department store. We could also think that a series of practical exercises with examples taken precisely from conventional media with regard to *miscalculation of sample size*, the *Fort effect* or the overestimation of low probabilities would create a breed of journalists able to resist the predictable traps when engaged in the rush for broadcasting information.

It is not too late to conceive ongoing training on this kind of subject for editorial boards that are already installed and experienced. Every professional who sees their environment change suddenly understands the need to train constantly; medics, researchers, technicians of all kinds, etc. Yet, their professional context pits journalists head on against the revolution of the cognitive market. It is a sign of weakness for them to conceive the need for ongoing training in order to be above ordinary logic.

Furthermore, if mechanisms of the cognitive market are hard to regulate from an authoritarian perspective, we can undoubtedly reduce the perverse effects of an unbridled information deregulation. It is in this sense that we must understand the initiative of the society *Pro Publica* headed by Paul Steiger, who was chief editor of the *Wall Street Journal*, to finance extensive investigations whose results are made available for traditional media. When realizing that market conditions no longer permitted the media to do research for long periods, this society began to render some kind of public service, made possible because billionaires Herb and Marion Sandler acted as patrons. As Poulet points out [POU 11, pp. 264–265]: "Public subventions for journals have perverse effects, it is known. By contrast, public financement and, why not, partially private financing, of public information could, if shared on a grand scale, be one of the ways to produce the information required for democratic life".

Finally, since some consider mass media as the fourth power, we can be astonished by the virtual anarchy that characterizes its modes of expression. This is probably quite unpleasant, but every power in democracy must be analyzed and defined. If we put aside the different hierarchies in the editorial rooms, where authority is not always exerted in terms of deontological criteria, the limits of media power become blurry.

This book is teeming with examples of mistakes made by conventional media without the application of any kind of sanction. One of the ways of undermining the democracy of the gullible would be to undertake a deep meditation about how to deal with the fourth power. It is neither feasible nor desirable to think in a political tutelage; that would be a huge democratic setback. By contrast, the possibility of being sanctioned by your own peers, as is the case in other professions where they have accepted the idea of self-regulation of power. Sportsmen, for instance, who often are much maligned, belong to a more deontologically organized group not that of journalists (has cyclist Lance Armstrong that paid the price?). As everyone can understand, the aim is to preserve everyone's freedom by restraining a power that has shown several times that it can become dictatorial.

Everybody makes mistakes, but when those mistakes perpetuate, they are expressed in accordance to predictable schemes and can have serious consequences for people or for economic interests, and then those mistakes become faults. It should be possible to peacefully discuss the way of limiting the probabilities that those faults appear in our public space.

Even if journalists are individuals just like the rest, their responsibility ranks above the average.

4.9. A new form of scientific communication

Just as every Saturday, you go out to do some shopping in your supermarket of choice; you are on the lookout for a good deal. You need to buy some coffee; one brand proposes a 33% reduction, while the other (that you like just as much) proposes an additional 50% of coffee. Which offer do you like the most?

According to an experimental study [CHE 12], it seems that most of us are persuaded that the second offer is more interesting, when they are *strictly* equivalent. In these conditions, 73% of buyers chose the second offer over the first offer. All the merchants of the world will know how to take advantage of this information. They will try to benefit from the banal and flawed state of our minds. We could call this technique *cognitive marketing* because it involves inciting an idea that will make a product more appealing for ordinary logic. Surely, there are more noble ambitions to conceive for these communication techniques that reckon with the natural propensities of our minds. We can convene them as a tool for defending methodical thinking on the cognitive market.

In many radio or television debates that talk about risk issues, paranormal phenomena, astrology or other adulterated products, we often have the impression that the experts are led to argumentative impasses from which they can no longer escape. These impasses may come from the perception of low probabilities, amazing coincidences, misunderstood proportionality ratios etc. the experts often come only with their expertise, thinking that will be enough. In a perfect world where arguments would be naturally assessed with regard to their relevance, that would certainly be enough. This is not the case, even less so in the current conditions of the cognitive market. If the bogus sometimes defeats the truth in the public space, it is because in certain situations with structures, certainly specific but rather frequent, it can count on the support of our mind's normal function. The mental illusions that come with it, and which we surrender to, can, as we have seen, disappear according to the way we change their mode of exposure.

I think that under current circumstances, those who define the characteristics of the democracy of the gullible justify the need for this cognitive marketing to give the public an expression of science as a tool that helps ordinary logic to recognize the quality of its argumentation and, therefore, to take a distance from deceptive reasoning. This does not call for lying and manipulation to convince, but only for realistically judging the way in which debates happen today in public space, and allow for open debate, even when faced with the natural propensities of our mind. How can we introduce neutral arguments and data that in public debate are almost systematically distorted by cognitive biases, used consciously or not for a militant purpose?

The aim is to create a foundation for a new way of communication; it would be necessary, if it is to be done right, to dedicate a whole book to the subject. I only want to suggest here that it is a feasible way of action with the virtue, in contrast with the required pedagogic adjustments that I mentioned in section 4.7, of having an immediate effect.

It is necessary, for the best course of action, to identify the most prominent elements of the activist's argumentation and those of them that are the most ingrained and that seem the most credible to the citizens who are wary of these technologies. In other words, it is a question of detecting what the cognitive products that are widely known in the market are. We must then determine the faulty cognitive foundation of these arguments and see how they can be presented so that exchanges on these questions are more reasonable.

For example, Gigerenzer [GIG 09, pp. 82–83] shows that communication with regard to detection of breast cancer can be done by means of very different presentations. We can say, on one hand, that detection through mammography reduces by 25% the risk of breast cancer deaths. This figure means that for every 1,000 screened women, three will die from breast cancer, while for 1,000 who were not, four will die (thus, 25% will be actually saved). It is fair to say today, on the other hand, that the reduction of risk equals one for every 1,000. Indeed, as we just saw it, a woman out of 1,000 will be saved due to a breast cancer detection test. It is easy to understand, depending on how they introduce information of this or that other manner. The impact, in terms of public opinion, will not be the same, yet none of these representations is a lie.

Those in charge of enlightenment have not become aware that their ineptitude in terms of cognitive marketing made them lose fragments of the market. It is true, that this market changed structurally and some of the rules that I tried to describe in this work only emerge through observation.

4.10. A new militancy

It is not enough that a cognitive proposition is correctly presented to be available in satisfactory manner for public space. The exposition of an idea in the cognitive market largely depends on the motivation of the suppliers and relays the *Olson Effect*. The Internet is, from this standpoint, a strange democracy; some vote thousands of times, others never. Thus, orthodox knowledge paradoxically finds itself on the minority side in many fields. I do not see the scientific world catching up with this problem and getting consequently involved step-by-step in this competition. I do not even think that it is desirable for the general interest, since this would necessarily rob precious time for the production of knowledge. Thus, what is missing, and which opens a path to finding solutions for this situation, is a relay network for orthodox knowledge. Such a network does exist but it is too weak; it is much more, at any rate, than the network which organized in the past the coordination of scholarly societies in our territory. The site of the National Council of Higher Education and Research identifies more than 119 scholarly societies today, while there were less than 1,000 in 1900. What is certainly more serious is that, since the year 2000, we have noticed an ageing of the members of scholarly societies and a lack of interest of the youngest categories for their activities. Maybe it is only a coincidence, but it turns out that this date also corresponds to the diffusion of the Internet network. This hypothesis is difficult to test, but we often have the impression that this network has taken charge of spreading scientific information (or intends to). One of the important stakes seems to me is to think of the manner in which these popular science networks can be reactivated. I think that teachers at elementary and secondary school could play a major role because they are competent and still benefit from a form of authority and trust necessary for such initiative. One of the chief solutions that we find for this problem is first of all micro social; it is by communicating with fellowmen, known individuals, that the feeling of mistrust can recede inch-by-inch. Several experiences have shown that the fact of having an emotional link with the broadcaster of some information, message or belief tends to give him more credibility. Shérif and Hovland [SHE 61] stress the fact that individuals tend to overrate the talents of individuals they are fond of, or that they love; on the other hand, they will underrate the talents of those whom they do not appreciate. That is why it is so important to give an almost familiar personification when possible, to the science speech in order to throw away the ghosts of a corrupted science, guilty of endless conflicts of interests and sold out to international capitalism. It is the time that every competent actor, at whatever level he is, undertook the battle of influence on the cognitive market in favor of the democracy of enlightenment and methodical thinking to send packing, everywhere, the scholars of illusion. Many of our contemporaries are currently aware of this flood of paradoxical credulity in contemporary societies; sometimes, they ask themselves "what can be done?". The answer is simple, you do not have to do more than militant believers, those who have the motivation to occupy the empty space that we leave in the information market; all you have to do is to find and elicit the motivation to answer them. There is no need for some to make a crusade out of this, just a sufficiently large number of individuals of good will think that enough is enough and it is time to answer back. Where? Everywhere. On blogs, forums, social networks … wherever the bogus takes advantage of the indifference of ordinary citizens. It is of central importance, since, as we have seen, the structuration of the information market has an impact on the undecided. Yet, we are all occasionally uncertain on a number of issues. If this new variety of militancy could take shape, it would prove this classic sentence wrong: every despotism always knows how to enjoy the apathy of the good people.

Conclusion

We all have personal beliefs, the man who wrote these lines, as much as the man or the woman who will read them. That is why I would like to clarify, so there is no misunderstanding, that the object of my commitment is not the believers but the beliefs.

As far as believers are concerned, they are discussed in this book and in almost everything that I have written on this subject; I know that their gullibility is not the result of stupidity or insincerity. I also think, essentially, that their firm belief is not the result of irrational forces, but simply of the fact they have reasons to believe. It does not mean that they are right for believing, but only that we have a better understanding of their illusions once we have attempted to rebuild the mental universe which is theirs.

As far as beliefs are concerned, some are amusing, but many can have terrible consequences. This is evident with regard to political or religious radicalisms; I will not offend the readers by giving examples of the like. This is also true of all the illusions which lead to ideological scenarios and that inspire, in certain individuals, mistrust or even a general loathing of the world in which we live in. I am not so sure that the western world deserves all this spitefulness, but that depends on your own point of view. At any rate, we certainly think that all these beliefs and the political demands that come along with them often put our country, and Europe especially, in situations of very disadvantageous competition with regard to other states where democracy is not a political path. If there is a fear, undoubtedly excessive, that pervades this book, it is to see our democracies brought down to their knees by their own demons ... to see the democracy of the gullible turn our world into a suburb forsaken by history.

Bibliography

[AJZ 83] AJZEN I., KRUGLANSKI A., "Bias and error in human judgement", *European Journal of Social Psychology*, vol. 13, pp. 1–49, 1983.

[ALB 03] ALBERT P.L., *Histoire de la presse*, PUF, 2003.

[ALL 47] ALLPORT G., POSTMAN L., *The Psychology of Rumor*, Henry Holt, New York, 1947.

[ANF 10] ANFOSSI C., *La sociologie au pays des croyances conspirationnistes – le théâtre du 11 Septembre*, mémoire de M2 inédit, Strasbourg, 2010.

[ARG 86] ARGOTE L., SEABRIGHT M.A., DYER L., "Individual versus group use of base-rate and individuating information", *Organisational Behavior and Human Decision Processes*, vol. 38, pp. 65–75, 1986.

[ATR 06] ATRAN S., "Les origines cognitives et évolutionnistes de la religion", in FUSSLAN G. (ed.), *Croyance, raison et déraison*, Odile Jacob, Paris, 2006.

[AUT 02] AUTRET M., "La brouillotique nous gagne", *Ecrire et éditer*, no. 39, p. 1, 2002.

[BAC 60] BACKAN P., "Response tendencies in attempts to generate random binary series", *American Journal of Psychology*, vol. 73, pp. 127–131, 1960.

[BAC 86] BACON F., *Novum organum*, PUF, Paris, 1986.

[BAI 82] BAIJENT M., LEIGH R., LINCOLN H., *L'énigme sacrée*, Pygmalion, Paris, 1982.

[BAU 08] BAUERLEIN M., *The Dumbest Generation*, Tarcher/Penguin, London, 2008.

[BEL 99] BÉLANGER M., *Sceptique Ascendant Sceptique*, Edition Stanké, Montreal, 1999.

[BIN 05] BINDÉ J., Vers les sociétés du savoir, Rapport Mondial de l'Unesco, Editions UNESCO, 2005.

[BOU 86] BOUCHAYER F., "Les usagers des médecines alternatives: itinéraires thérapeutiques, culturels, existentiels", Revue française des affaires sociales, pp. 105–115, April 1986.

[BOU 90] BOUDON R., L'Art de se persuader, Fayard, Paris, 1990.

[BOU 94] BOUDON R., CLAVELIN M., Le relativisme est-il résistible?, PUF, Paris, 1994.

[BOU 08] BOUDON R., Le relativisme, PUF, Paris, 2008.

[BOU 12] BOUDON R., Croire et savoir, PUF, Paris, 2012.

[BOV 53] BOVARD E.W., "Conformity to social norms in stable an temporary groups", Science, vol. 117, pp. 361–363, 1953.

[BOY 86] BOY D., MICHELAT G., "Croyances aux parasciences: dimensions sociales et culturelles", La Revue Française de Sociologie, vol. 27, pp. 175–204, 1986.

[BOY 03] BOY D., "L'évolution des opinions sur les biotechnologies dans l'Union européenne", Revue Internationale de Politique Comparée, vol. 10, no. 2, pp. 207–218, 2003.

[BRO 89] BROCH H., Le paranormal, le Seuil, Paris, 1989.

[BRO 97] BRONNER G., L'incertitude, PUF, Paris, 1997.

[BRO 03] BRONNER G., L'empire des croyances, PUF, Paris, 2003.

[BRO 06] BRONNER G., Vie et mort des croyances collectives, Hermann, Paris, 2006.

[BRO 07a] BRONNER G., L'empire de l'erreur – Eléments de sociologie cognitive, PUF, Paris, 2007.

[BRO 07b] BRONNER G., "La résistance au darwinisme: croyances et raisonnements", La Revue Française de Sociologie, vol. 3, pp. 587–607, 2007.

[BRO 07c] BRONNER G., Coïncidences – Nos représentations du hasard, Vuibert, Paris, 2007.

[BRO 10a] BRONNER G., The Future of Collective Beliefs, Bardwell Press, Oxford, 2010.

[BRO 10b] BRONNER G., "Ondes et croyances", La Revue des Deux Mondes, pp. 51–75, March 2010.

[BRO 11] BRONNER G., "Ce qu'Internet fait à la diffusion des croyances", Revue Européenne de Sciences Sociales, vol. 49–1, pp. 35–60, 2011.

[CAM 02] CAMPION-VINCENT V., RENARD J.-B., Légendes urbaines, Payot, Paris, 2002.

[CAM 05] CAMPION-VINCENT V., *La société parano*, Payot, Paris, 2005.

[CAR 08] CARR N., *The Big Switch: Rewiring the World, from Edison to Google*, W. W. Norton & Company, New York, 2008.

[CAR 10] CARDON D., *La démocratie Internet*, Seuil, Paris, 2010.

[CAS 78] CASSCELLS W., SCHOENBERGER A., GRAYBOYS T., "Interpretation by physicians of clinical laboratory results", *New England Journal of Medicine*, vol. 299, pp. 999–1000, 1978.

[CHA 80] CHAIKEN S., "Heuristic versus systematic information processing and the use of source versus message cue in persuasion", *Journal of Personality and Social Psychology*, vol. 39, no. 5, pp. 752–766, 1980.

[CHA 05] CHARPIER F., *L'obsession du complot*, François Bourin, Paris, 2005.

[CHE 07] CHERKAOUI M., *Good Intentions – Max Weber and the Paradox of Unintended Consequences*, Bardwell Press, Oxford, 2007.

[CHE 12] CHEN H., MARMORSTEIN H., TSIROS M. *et al.*, "When more is less: the impact of base value neglect on consumer preferences for bonus packs over price discounts", *Journal of Marketing*, vol. 76, no. 4, pp. 64–77, 2012.

[COH 81] COHEN L.J., "Can human irrationality be experimentally demonstrated?", *Behaviorial and Brain Sciences*, vol. 4, pp. 317–370, 1981.

[COH 02] COHEN D., Terrorisme: la pauvreté n'est pas coupable, *Le Monde*, 7 October 2002.

[COS 96] COSMIDES L., TOOBY J., "Are humans good intuitive statisticians after all? Rethinking some conclusions from the literature on judgement under uncertainty", *Cognition*, vol. 58, pp. 1–73, 1996.

[CRE 81] CRENSHAW M., "The cause of terrorism", *Comparative Politics*, vol. 13, pp. 379–399, 1981.

[CUN 89] CUNIOT A., *Incroyable... mais faux!*, L'horizon chimérique, Bordeaux, 1989.

[DEF 95] DEFALVARD H., *Essais sur le marché*, Paris, Syros, 1995.

[DOG 05] DOGAN M. (ed.), *Political Mistrust and the Discrediting of Politicians*, Brill, Leyde and Boston, 2005.

[DON 08] DONNAT O., Pratiques culturelles des Français à l'ère numérique, La Découverte/Ministère de la Culture et de la Communication, Paris, 2008.

[DRO 97] DROZDA-SENKOWSKA E. (ed.), *Les Pièges du raisonnement*, Retz, Paris, 1997.

[DRU 69] DRUCKER P., *The Age of Discontinuity. Guidelines to Our Changing Society*, Harper & Row, New York, 1969.

[DUV 02] DUVAL M., *Un ethnologue au Mandarom*, PUF, Paris, 2002.

[EC 79] EUROPEAN COMMISSION, Les attitudes du public européen face au développement scientifique et technique, available at: ec.europa.eu/public_opinion_archives/ebs/ebs_11_fr.pdf, 1979.

[EAG 06] EAGER T., MUSSO C., "Why did the World Trade Center collapse: science, engineering and speculation", *The Journal of the Minerals, Metals and Materials Society*, vol. 53, no. 12, pp. 8–11, 2006.

[EFS 06] EUROPEAN FOOD SAFETY AUTHORITY (EFSA), "Opinion of the scientific panel on food additives, flavourings, processing aids and materials in contact with food (AFC) on a request from the Commission related to a new long term carcinogenecity study of aspartame", *The EFSA Journal*, vol. 356, pp. 1–44, 2006.

[ERN 06] ERNER G., *La société des victimes*, La Découverte, Paris, 2006.

[ETC 05] ETCHEGOIN M.-F., ARON M., *Le bûcher de Toulouse -D'Allègre à Baudis Histoire d'une mystification*, Grasset, Paris, 2005.

[ETI 05] ETIENNE B., *Les combattants suicidaires*, L'aube, Paris, 2005.

[FIS 84a] FISCHHOFF B., "For those condemned to study the past: heuristics and biases in hindsight", in TVERSKY A., KAHNEMAN D., SLOVIC P. (eds), *Judgment Under Uncertainty: Heuristics and Biaises*, Cambridge University Press, Cambridge, pp. 201–208, 1984.

[FIS 84b] FISKE, TAYLOR S., *Social Cognition*, Random House, New York, 1984.

[FLI 10] FLICHY P., *Le sacre de l'amateur*, Seuil, Paris, 2010.

[FOR 55] FORT C., *Le livre des damnés*, Les Éditions des Deux Rives, Paris, 1955.

[FRI 93] FRIEDRICH J., "Primary detection and minimization strategies in social cognition: a reinterpretation of confirmation bias phenomena", *Psychological Review*, vol. 100, no. 2, pp. 298–319, 1993.

[FUE 02] FUENTÈS P., "Camille Flammarion et les forces naturelles inconnues", in BENSAUDE-VINCENT B., BLONDEL C. (eds), *Des savants face à l'occulte 1870-1940*, Editions La Découverte, Paris, pp. 105–124, 2002.

[GAL 65] GALIFRET Y. (ed.), *Le crépuscule des magiciens*, Editions rationalistes, Paris, 1965.

[GIG 09] GIGERENZER G., *Penser le risque: Apprendre à vivre dans l'incertitude*, Markus Haller, Paris, 2009.

[GIR 89] GIROTTO V., LEGRENZI P., "Mental representation and hypothetico-deductive reasoning: The case of the thog problem", *Psychological Research*, vol. 51, no. 3, pp. 129–135, 1989.

[GRI 83] GRIGGS, NEWSTEAD S., "The source of intuitive errors in Wason's THOG problem", *British Journal of Psychology*, vol. 74, no. 4, pp. 451–459, 1983.

[HAZ 10] HAZELL R., WORTHY M., GLOVER M., *The Impact of the Freedom of Information Act on Central Government in the UK*, Palgrave Macmillan, Londres, 2010.

[HEL 05] HELLER D., "Taking a closer look: hard science and the collapse of the Word Trade Center", *Garlic and Grass*, vol. 6, available at: www.garlicandgrass.org/issue6/Dave_Heller.cfm, 2005.

[ING 03] INGELHART R. (ed.), *Human Values and Social Change*, Brill, Boston, MA, 2003.

[JAM 03] JAMAIN S., BETANCUR C., GIROS B. *et al.*, "La génétique de l'autisme", *Médecine/Science*, vol. 19, pp. 1081–1090, 2003.

[JOU 00] JOURDAN B., *Les imposteurs de la génétique*, Le Seuil, Paris, 2000.

[JOU 07] JOURDAIN B., "Remous autour d'un test génétique", *Science et pseudo-sciences*, vol. 276, pp. 26–27, 2007.

[JOL 15] JOLY P.-B., KAUFNANN A., Introduction to citizen participation in science and technology, available at: www.icipast.org/download /CD%20CIPAST%20in% 20Active/cipast/en/design_2.htm, 2015.

[KAP 95] KAPFERER J.-N., *Rumeurs*, le Seuil, Paris, 1995.

[KEE 07] KEEN A., *The Cult of the Amateur*, Bantam, New York, 2007.

[KHO 06] KHOSROKHAVAR F., *Quand Al-Qaïda parle*, Grasset, Paris, 2006.

[KRI 10] KRIVINE J.-P., "Vaccination: les alertes et leurs conséquences", *Science et pseudoscience*, vol. 291, pp. 117–118, 2010.

[KRU 07] KRUEGER A., *What Makes a Terrorist: Economics and the Roots of Terrorism*, Princeton University Press, 2007.

[LAG 05] LAGRANGE P., *La guerre des mondes a-t-elle eu lieu?*, Robert Laffont, Paris, 2005.

[LAU 80] LAUNIÈRE DE C., "Aux yeux de la science officielle, la parapsychologie n'a pas encore fait ses preuves", *Québec Science*, vol. 19, no. 1, pp. 17–21, 1980.

[LED 09] LEDOUX A., "Vidéos en ligne: la preuve par l'image?", *Esprit*, pp. 95–107, March–April 2009.

[LEQ 02] LEQUÈVRE F., "L'astrologie", in MAHRIC (ed.), *Guide critique de l'extraordinaire*, Les arts libéraux, Bordeaux, 2002.

[LOR 03] LORIOL M., "Faire exister une maladie controversée", *Sciences sociales et santé*, vol. 4, pp. 5–33, 2003.

[MAN 98] MANSELL R., WEHN U., *Knowledge Societies: Information Technology for Sustainable Development*, United Nations Commission on Science and Technology for Development, Oxford University Press, New York, 1998.

[MAR 10] MARCHETTI D., *Quand la santé devient médiatique. Les logiques de production de l'information dans la presse*, PUG, 2010.

[MCK 99] MCKAY B., BAR-NATAN D., BAR-HILIEL M. *et al.*, "Solving the Bible Code Puzzle", *Statistical Science*, vol. 14, pp. 150–173, 1999.

[MIL 88] MILL J.S., *Système de logique, Mardaga, Bruxelles*, 1988.

[MOL 07] MOLE P., "Les théories conspirationnistes autour du 11 septembre", *Science et pseudoscience*, no. 279, pp. 4–13, 2007.

[MOR 02] MOREL C., *Les décisions absurdes*, Gallimard, Paris, 2002.

[MOR 11] MORIN H., Les glorieuses incertitudes de la science – Le doute scientifique, une attitude exemplaine, available at: www.resistanceinventene. blogspot.com, 25 September 2011.

[NAT 04] NATIONAL COMMISION, *The 9/11 Commission Report: Find Report of the National Commission on Terrorist Attacks on the United states*, W.W. Norton, New York, 2004.

[NIS 80] NISBETT R.E., ROSS L., *Human Inference: Strategies and Shortcomings of Social Judgement*, Prentice-Hall, Englewood Cliffs, N.J., 1980.

[OBR 90] O'BRIEN D. *et al.*, "Source of difficulty in deductive reasoning: the THOG task", *The Quarterly Journal of Experimental Psychology*, vol. 42, no. 2, pp. 329–351, 1990.

[OLI 00] OLIVIER HOUDÉ O., ZAGO L., MELLET E. *et al.*, "Shifting from the perceptual brain to the logical brain: the neural impact of cognitive inhibition training", *Journal of Cognitive Neuroscience*, vol. 12, no. 5, pp. 721–728, 2000.

[OLS 78] OLSON M., *La logique de l'action collective*, PUF, Paris, 1978.

[PAR 11] PARISER E., *The Filter Bubble: What the Internet Is Hiding from You*, Penguin Press, London, 2011.

[PER 09] PERRIN A., "Ondes électromagnétiques: comment s'y retrouver dans l'information?", *SPS*, vol. 285, pp. 10–16, 2009.

[PIA 95] PIATELLI P.M., *La réforme du jugement ou comment ne plus se tromper*, Odile Jacob, Paris, 1995.

[PIA 06] PIATELLI P.M., RAUDE J., *Choix, décisions et préférences*, Odile Jacob, Paris, 2006.

[POU 11] POULET B., *La fin des journaux et l'avenir de l'information*, Gallimard, Paris, 2011.

[PRE 48] PRESTON M.G., BARATTA P., "An experimental study of the auction – value of an uncertain uncome", *American Journal of Psychology*, vol. 61, pp. 183–193, 1948.

[PRE 98] PRELEC D., "The probability weighting function", *Econometrica*, vol. 47, pp. 313–327, 1998.

[REN 10] RENARD J.-B., "Croyances fantastiques et rationalité", *L'Année Sociologique*, vol. 60–1, pp. 115–135, 2010.

[REN 11] RENARD J.-B., *Le merveilleux*, CNRS Editions, Paris, 2011.

[ROS 75] ROSS L., LEEPER R., HUBBARD, "Perseverance in self-perception and social perception: biased attributional processes in the debriefing paradigm", *Journal of Personality and Social Psychology*, vol. 32, pp. 880–892, 1975.

[ROS 80] ROSS L., LEEPER R., "The perseverance of beliefs: empirical and normative considerations", in SHWEDER R.A., FISKE D.W. (eds), *New Directions for Methodology of Behavioral Science: Faillible Judgement in Behavioral Research*, Jossey-Bass, San Francisco, pp. 79–93, 1980.

[ROS 06] ROSENVALLON P., *La contre-démocratie, la politique à l'âge de la défiance*, Seuil, Paris, 2006.

[RUB 02] RUBY C.L., "Are terrorists mentally deranged?", *Analysis of Social Issues and Public Policy*, vol. 2, pp. 15–26. 2002.

[SAG 04] SAGEMAN M., *Understanding Terror Networks*, University of Pennsylvania Press, Philadelphia, 2004.

[SAU 12] SAUVAYRE R., *Croire en l'incroyable*, PUF, Paris, 2012.

[SER 07] SÉRALINI G.-E., CELLIER D., SPIROUX DE VENDOMOIS J., "New analysis of a rat feeding study with a genetically modified maize reveals signs of hepatorenal toxicity", *Archives of Environmental Contamination and Toxicology*, pp. 596–602, 2007.

[SHE 61] SHÉRIF M., HOVLAND C.I., *Social Judgment*, University Press, Yales, New Haven, 1961.

[SHT 12] SHTULMAN A., VALCARCEL J., "Scientific knowledge suppresses but does not supplant earlier intuitions", *Cognition*, vol. 124, no. 2, pp. 209–215, 2012.

[SIM 59] SIMON H., "Theories and decision-making in economics and behavioral science", *American Economic Review*, vol. 49, no. 3, pp. 253–283, 1959.

[SIM 63] SIMON H., "Economics and psychology", in KOCH S. (ed.), *Psychology: A Study of Science, 6th ed.*, McGraw Hill, New York, 1963.

[SIM 01] SIMONS A., *The Story Factor*, Basic Books, New York, 2001.

[SLO 84] SLOVIC P., FISCHHOFF B., LICHTENSTEIN S., "Facts versus fears: understanding perceived risk", in TVERSKY A., KAHNEMAN D., SLOVIC P. (eds), *Judgment Under Uncertainty: Heuristics and Biaises*, Cambridge University Press, Cambridge, pp. 464–489, 1984.

[SOF 06] SOFFRITI M. *et al.*, "First experimental demonstration of the multipotential carcinogenic effects of aspartame administered in the feed to Sprague-Dawley rats", *Env. Health Perspect.*, vol. 114, pp. 379–385, 2006.

[SPE 89] SPERBER D., WILSON D., *La pertinence – communication et cognition*, Editions de Minuit, Paris, 1989.

[STE 94] STEHR N., *Knowledge Societies: the Transformation of Labour, Property and Knowledge in Contemporary Society*, Sage, London, 1994.

[STO 99] STOCZKOWSKI W., *Des hommes, des dieux et des extraterrestres*, Flammarion, Paris, 1999.

[STU 84] STUPPLE D., "Mahatmas and space brothers: the ideologies of alleged contact with extraterrestrials", *Journal of American Culture*, vol. 7, nos. 1–2, pp. 131–139, 1984.

[SUN 06] SUNSTEIN C.R., *Infotopia: How Many Minds Produce Knowledge*, Oxford University Press, Londres, Oxford, 2006.

[TAG 05] TAGUIEFF P.-A., *La foire aux illuminés*, Mille et une nuit, Paris, 2005.

[TAP 08] TAPSCOTT D., *Grown Up Digital*, McGraw-Hill, New York, 2008.

[THO 04] THOUVEREZ L., "Mr Azn@r, par T" Manipulations informatives et révolte SMS du 11 au 14 mars 2004 en Espagne", *Revue de Civilisation Contemporaine de l'Université de Bretagne Occidentale*, vol. 4, available at: https://amnis.revues.org/710, 2004.

[TOC 92] TOCQUEVILLE ALEXIS DE, *De la démocratie en Amérique*, 2nd ed., Gallimard, Paris, 1992.

[TVE 71] TVERSKY A., KAHNEMAN D., "Belief in the law of small numbers", *Psychological Bulletin*, vol. 2, pp. 105–110, 1971.

[TVE 74] TVERSKY A., KAHNEMAN D., "Judgment under uncertainty: heuristics and biaises", *Science*, vol. 185, pp. 1124–1131, 1974.

[TVE 84a] TVERSKY A., KAHNEMAN D., "Evidential impact of base rates", in TVERSKY A., KAHNEMAN D., SLOVIC P. (eds), *Judgment Under Uncertainty: Heuristics and Biaises*, Cambridge University Press, Cambridge, pp. 153–160, 1984.

[TVE 84b] TVERSKY A., KAHNEMAN D., SLOVIC P. (eds), *Judgment Under Uncertainty: Heuristics and Biaises*, Cambridge University Press, Cambridge, 1984.

[TVE 86] TVERSKY A., KAHNEMAN D., "The framing of decisions and the psychology of choice", *Science*, vol. 211, pp. 453–458, 1986.

[UNE 05] UNESCO., Towards knowledge societies, UNESCO Publishing, 2005.

[VAI 07] VAIN P., "Trends in GM crop, food and feed safety literature", *Nature Biotechnology*, vol. 25, no. 6, p. 624, 2007.

[VIE 96] VIENNOT L., *Raisonner en physique. La part du sens commun*, De Boeck, Bruxelles, 1996.

[WAS 66] WASON P.C., "Reasoning", in FOSS B.M. (ed.), *New Horizons in Psychology*, 1st ed., Penguin, Londres, pp. 135–151, 1966.

[WAS 77] WASON P.C., "Self-contradiction", in JOHNSON-LAIRD P.N., WASON P.C. (eds), *Thinking: Reading in Cognitive Science*, Cambridge University Press, Cambridge, pp. 114–128, 1977.

[WAT 78] WATZLAWICK P., *La réalité de la réalité*, le Seuil, Paris, 1978.

[WIT 94] WITZUM D., RIPS E., ROSENBERG Y., "Sequences of equidistant letters in Genesis", *Statistical Science*, vol. 9, pp. 429–438, 1994.

Index

Other titles from

in

Information Systems, Web and Pervasive Computing

2015

ARDUIN Pierre-Emmanuel, GRUNDSTEIN Michel,
ROSENTHAL-SABROUX Camille
Information and Knowledge System

BÉRANGER Jérôme
Medical Information Systems Ethics

IAFRATE Fernando
From Big Data to Smart Data

POMEROL Jean-Charles, EPELBOIN Yves, THOURY Claire
MOOCs

SALLES Maryse
Decision-Making and the Information System

2014

DINET Jérôme
Information Retrieval in Digital Environments

HÉNO Raphaële, CHANDELIER Laure
3D Modeling of Buildings: Outstanding Sites

2011

BANOS Arnaud, THÉVENIN Thomas
Geographical Information and Urban Transport Systems

DAUPHINÉ André
Fractal Geography

LEMBERGER Pirmin, MOREL Mederic
Managing Complexity of Information Systems

STOCKINGER Peter
Introduction to Audiovisual Archives

STOCKINGER Peter
Digital Audiovisual Archives

VENTRE Daniel
Cyberwar and Information Warfare

2010

BONNET Pierre
Enterprise Data Governance

BRUNET Roger
Sustainable Geography

CARREGA Pierre
Geographical Information and Climatology

CAUVIN Colette, ESCOBAR Francisco, SERRADJ Aziz
Thematic Cartography – 3-volume series
Thematic Cartography and Transformations – volume 1
Cartography and the Impact of the Quantitative Revolution – volume 2
New Approaches in Thematic Cartography – volume 3

LANGLOIS Patrice
Simulation of Complex Systems in GIS

MATHIS Philippe
Graphs and Networks – 2nd edition

THÉRIAULT Marius, DES ROSIERS François
Modeling Urban Dynamics

2009

BONNET Pierre, DETAVERNIER Jean-Michel, VAUQUIER Dominique
Sustainable IT Architecture: the Progressive Way of Overhauling Information Systems with SOA

PAPY Fabrice
Information Science

RIVARD François, ABOU HARB Georges, MERET Philippe
The Transverse Information System

ROCHE Stéphane, CARON Claude
Organizational Facets of GIS

VENTRE Daniel
Information Warfare

2008

BRUGNOT Gérard
Spatial Management of Risks

FINKE Gerd
Operations Research and Networks

GUERMOND Yves
Modeling Process in Geography

KANEVSKI Michael
Advanced Mapping of Environmental Data

MANOUVRIER Bernard, LAURENT Ménard
Application Integration: EAI, B2B, BPM and SOA

PAPY Fabrice
Digital Libraries

Printed and bound by CPI Group (UK) Ltd, Croydon, CR0 4YY

27/10/2024

14580240-0005